Collins
LITTLE BOOKS

G000244094

IRISH
WHISKEY

Gary Quinn

HarperCollins Publishers
Westerhill Road
Bishopbriggs
Glasgow
G64 2QT

First Edition 2020

Reprint 10 9 8 7 6 5 4 3 2 1

© HarperCollins Publishers 2020

Text © Gary Quinn 2020

ISBN 978-0-00-834066-7

Collins® is a registered trademark
of HarperCollins Publishers Limited

www.collins.co.uk

A catalogue record for this book is
available from the British Library

Typeset by
Davidson Publishing Solutions

Printed and bound in China by
RR Donnelley APS Co Ltd

MIX
Paper from
responsible sources
FSC™ C007454

This book is produced from independently certified FSC™ paper
to ensure responsible forest management.

For more information visit: www.harpercollins.co.uk/green

Contents

About the Author

Gary Quinn is an award-winning travel writer and editor. His writing on whiskey has featured in national print and digital media and his former column, Barfly, which told stories from great traditional Irish bars and was published in *The Irish Times*, won Best New Irish Blog at the Travel Media Awards in 2016. After more than a decade in traditional editorial newsrooms he moved into brand content, where he has led multiple award-winning commercial media campaigns. His work, specializing in telling distinctly Irish stories about major national and international brands, won the INMA Global Media Award for Best Native Campaign in both 2017 and 2018.

His first whiskey was a glass of Powers, enjoyed at the beginning of a decade tending bar. Since then, he has travelled Ireland recording the stories of the bar staff, distillers, business owners, and customers that are the lifeblood of the Irish whiskey industry. His occasional podcast, Books in Bars, features writers drinking whiskey in their favourite pubs.

What this book covers

In this book I have tried to capture the personality of Ireland's working distilleries and independent brands. In a time of rapid growth for the sector I want to champion Irish whiskey and allow as many people as possible to enjoy the journey it's on.

The book is as much a travel guide to Ireland's new distillery network as it is to the whiskeys they produce. In reading it, you should get a picture of the people, the places, and the products they have created. It should give you a comprehensive overview of Irish whiskey and the knowledge to choose a whiskey that matches your own personality and flavour preferences.

The first part of the book provides the story of each of the working distilleries and, where it exists, details their core range. Not all of the working distilleries are selling their own brand yet. Some of the younger distilleries have chosen not to use sourced whiskey from other distilleries, deciding instead to allow their own spirit to mature before putting their name to it.

The second part of the book is designed to celebrate the art of independent blending. Not all Irish whiskey brands have their own distillery, or ever intend to open one. This section introduces you to some of those independent brands who only source whiskey from distilleries to blend a new whiskey and outlines why their independence matters.

Irish whiskey is incredibly good fun and the people who drive it are passionate and full of life. I hope this book helps you meet them and get to enjoy what they make.

Introduction

If you're looking for a dramatic pursuit, lose yourself in the story of Irish whiskey. It has all the elements of a great saga: poor beginnings, roaring success, sudden decline, a romantic back story, and back-from-the-brink re-invention – while bursting at the seams with plot twists.

While it's gratifying to reflect on Irish whiskey's past, with its sixth-century beginnings, eighteenth-century rapid growth, and nineteenth-century global dominance of the spirits sector, what's happening now in the twenty-first century is incredibly exciting.

The Irish whiskey industry has suddenly exploded. The number of distilleries now in operation (twenty-six at the time of writing), as well as those planned to open, have taken the country by surprise, re-invigorating an industry that was for so long wrapped up in the fortunes of just a handful of distilleries. In 2010 there were only four whiskey distilleries in operation in Ireland: Midleton Distillery in County Cork, Old Bushmills in County Antrim, Kilbeggan in County Westmeath, and Cooley in County Louth.

These large-scale operations, each today owned by some of the biggest names in the global drinks industry, re-invented, fought for, and protected a category that was long in decline. In some cases, like with Irish Distillers' re-invention of Jameson, they created global whiskey brands that introduced a whole new generation of drinkers to Irish whiskey. While the latest chapter in the Irish whiskey story is all about the rise of independent craft distilling and bonding, the decades of work still being undertaken by the big distilleries is truly inspiring.

In 2018 Ireland exported 10.7 million cases of whiskey. This is an increase of some four million cases since 2010 and the sector is now said to be the fastest-growing whiskey category in the world. While it is still a long way behind the dominance of Scotch on the international market, the rapid growth in demand from new and old Irish whiskey fans, coupled with the Irish industry's ability to provide greater product innovation and choice, suggests that the sector's ambition is not misplaced.

Old whiskey from new distilleries

But we're not there yet. A lot of the whiskey brands in this book are from distilleries which are very young. They have all distilled their own spirit but many are yet to reach maturation. While you can sell Irish whiskey once it reaches three years old, it's quite rare to do so. As each of the new distilleries wait for their own spirit to mature, many of them have released brands using sourced whiskey from the existing distilleries. This is not a bad thing. The whiskey that is being used is generally of excellent quality and it creates a challenge for Irish whiskey blenders to use their skills to conjure flavours and combinations that genuinely stand out from the crowd. Their choice of source whiskey in terms of age and type, the barrel it is then extra-matured in, and the additional maturation time, determines the future of a brand. Consequently, the role of the master blender is an incredibly important one.

The whiskey business is also incredibly expensive. It can be many years, even decades, before any profit can be reclaimed. So the opportunity to sell a high-quality brand under the distillery name in advance of their own spirit being ready is crucial. As you visit distilleries, you will find that many also produce their own gin and vodka, creating a surge of popularity in these products that has been very positive. As gin and vodka have a very short production cycle, they help bolster the much slower production cycle of the whiskey. A third category you'll discover is poitín, a sometimes overlooked traditional distilled spirit that is slowly regaining an appreciation here.

Rise of the independents

A strong independent industry is key and it's that which is the new character in the Irish whiskey story. When the first casks were filled at Dingle Distillery in the winter of 2012, that distillery was leading the way in creating a new generation of whiskey distilleries. In the few short years since then, more than twenty new distilleries have begun production all across Ireland, North and South. This has created not just an industry but an entire movement, stuffed with personality and passion.

In towns, cities, and villages across the island, people from all walks of life suddenly find themselves wrapped up in the complicated business of whiskey. The most exciting part is watching so many young people being trained as coopers, distillers, blenders, and ambassadors – career paths that were rarely heard of ten years ago, owing to the scarcity of demand. The ambition of the industry has created an entirely new set of career opportunities, and not just for Irish people. As you tour the country's distilleries, expect to hear American, Australian, European, Asian, and, of course, Scottish accents ripple through warehouses and still rooms. People from all over the whiskey world have brought their expertise here and Irish whiskey is all the better for it as it prepares to play a bigger role than ever on the global whiskey stage.

What is Irish Whiskey?

A Beginner's Guide

In general, Irish whiskey tends towards smooth, sweet flavours and is often referred to as being easy to drink. Unlike Scotch, it does not usually have a smoky, peated flavour, although it can use peat and still be considered Irish whiskey. There are a small number of popular peated Irish whiskeys on the market, such as Kilbeggan's Connemara Peated Single Malt.

To be called Irish whiskey, the spirit must be distilled in Ireland, North or South, and the distilled spirit then matured for at least three years in wooden casks. People often add a day to that age reference for dramatic effect but three years is the legal minimum.

Irish whiskey can be double- or triple-distilled. Triple distillation is very common with Irish whiskey but double distillation is just as valid. The third distillation is said to add to the feeling of smoothness in the taste.

There are four types of Irish whiskey: malt whiskey, pot still whiskey, grain whiskey, and blended Irish whiskey.

Single Malt Irish Whiskey

In popular culture, the idea of a single malt is often widely understood to reference a sign of excellence but, in fact, it simply refers to the type of whiskey it is. The single in the name refers to the fact that it is made in a single distillery, while the malt refers to the fact that it contains 100 per cent malt barley, as well as water and yeast. It can be peated or unpeated and has a full and pleasant oily texture with a smooth, sweet, and malty finish. It is distilled in a pot still. Popular examples include **Dingle Single Malt**, **Teeling Single Malt**, and **Bushmills Single Malt**.

Single Pot Still Irish Whiskey

Single pot still whiskey is native to Ireland. It emerged in the late 1700s as a way of avoiding a tax on the use of malt. Pot still whiskey uses a combination of malted and unmalted barley. The unmalted part creates a spicy flavour and a creamy texture that allows it to stand apart from the flavour of single malt whiskey. It is distilled in a pot still. Some of the most popular Irish whiskey brands are single pot still whiskey and include **Redbreast**, **Green Spot**, and **Powers John's Lane**.

Single Grain Irish Whiskey

Irish grain whiskey must have a malt barley component in its recipe, but only up to a maximum of 30 per cent. The remainder can be a combination of unmalted grains such as maize, wheat, or barley. It is distilled in a column still and can be double- or triple-distilled. Popular examples of Irish grain whiskey include **Kilbeggan Single Grain**, **Powerscourt Distillery's Fercullen 10-year-old Single Grain**, and **Teeling's Single Grain**.

Blended Irish Whiskey

Blended Irish whiskey is a combination of two or more of the pot still, malt, and grain whiskeys. Generally, the lighter grain whiskey is combined with the heavier malt or pot still to create a new blend or flavour profile. It can also be a combination of all three styles, although this is rare. **Tullamore D.E.W.** is a great example of all three styles being combined to create an incredibly popular brand. **Bushmills Original** is a blend of their triple-distilled malt whiskey and a lighter grain whiskey.

Additives

The colour of Irish whiskey comes from the cask it is matured in. However, in order to allow consistency in the colour of a brand over time, the caramel colouring E150 is permitted. Although named after a flavour (caramel) this is a colouring only and has no flavour. It is the only additive which is permitted.

Wood, spirit, and maturation

Maturation warehouses are incredibly special places. Stacked to the ceiling with wooden casks slowly maturing new spirit into whiskey, they release a rich aroma that simply can't be bottled. This is the fabled angel's share; that part of the spirit that evaporates through the wood as it matures. The air in these warehouses is heavy with a sweet perfume that escapes through the wood of the cask or barrel as the wood "breathes". It's a wonderful alchemy that not only matures the spirit, allowing it to become whiskey, but also creates an incredible range of flavour profiles, depth of colour, and aromas.

Irish whiskey must be matured in wood and in the majority of cases that wood is oak, American Oak to be precise. Since, in the USA, there is a strict policy of using only new, unseasoned oak to make bourbon there is a ready supply of ex-bourbon casks for the Irish whiskey market.

The time spent maturing that bourbon will have stripped some of the minerals from the wood that create flavour, but the bourbon in turn will have passed its own flavour properties back into the wood, and they then get transferred into the new spirit, maturing into Irish whiskey.

Irish whiskey makers also use casks that have previously stored other drinks, such as sherry or port. Each of these will have left their own signature on the wood and this too will be transferred into the new spirit. Throughout this book you will find references to the type of cask the whiskey is matured or "finished" in. Irish whiskey has to mature for at least three years in cask but it is often much longer. Once mature, a whiskey can then be "finished" in another cask or barrel, to impart new flavour profiles. Different wood types can also be introduced at this stage.

The new make spirit that goes into a cask is a clear liquid. Its final identity, once it matures, is determined by the chemical reactions that occur between the wood of the cask and the spirit itself. Once bottled, ageing stops and the whiskey is complete but, until then, it's a wonderfully slow and exciting part of the whiskey-making process.

Anyone who journeys down the whiskey path is likely to become fascinated by this process, not least because it is an act of trust between the distiller and nature itself. The distiller and blender understand the process, choose the type of wood, and have an expectation of the result, but they can rarely predict the outcome with 100 per cent certainty. They simply have to wait and let the wood do its work.

Numbers in **bold** indicate the page
where the property can be found

*Atlantic
Ocean*

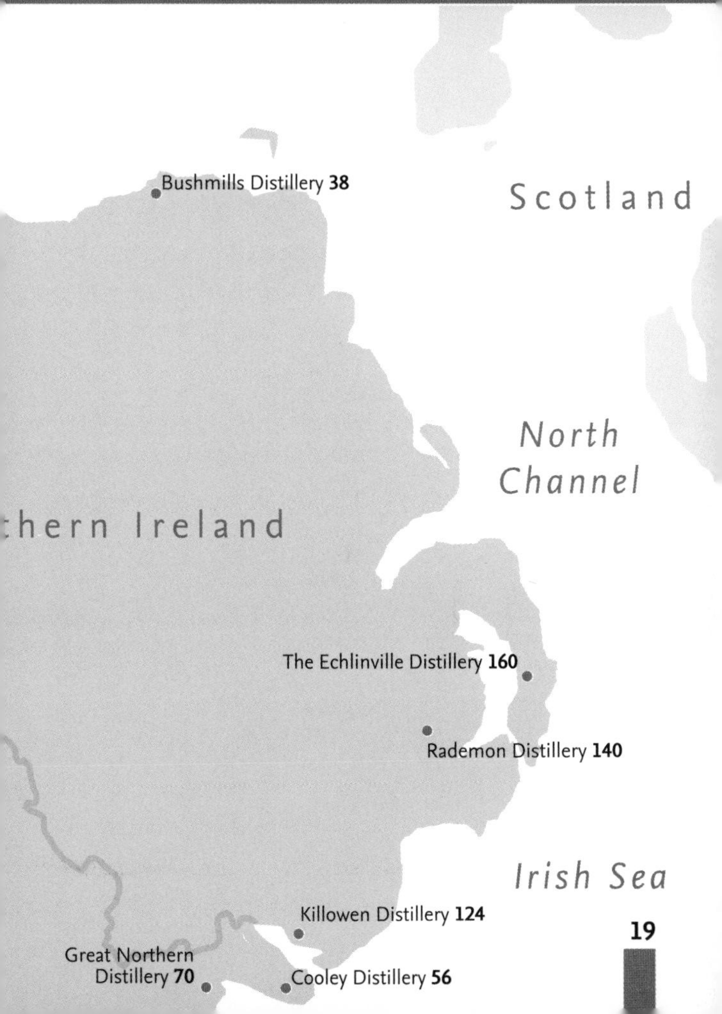

Bushmills Distillery **38**

Scotland

North
Channel

thern Ireland

The Echlinville Distillery **160**

Rademon Distillery **140**

Irish Sea

Killowen Distillery **124**

Great Northern
Distillery **70**

Cooley Distillery **56**

West Central Ireland

Achill Island Distillery **28**

Atlantic Ocean

Lough Measc Distillery **126**

Numbers in **bold** indicate the page
where the property can be found

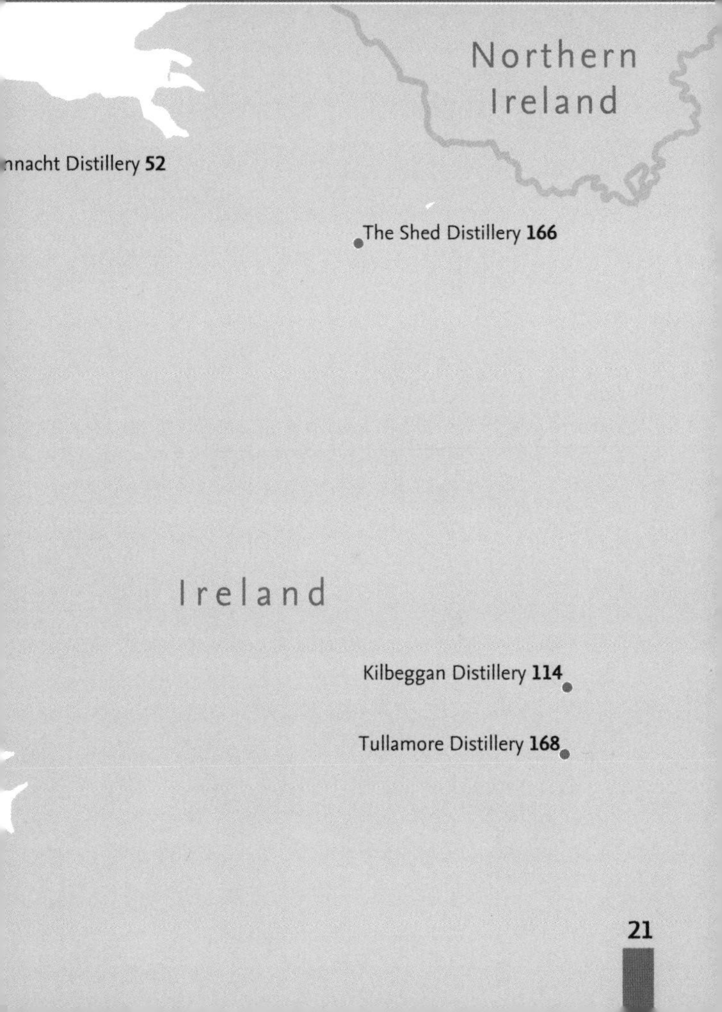
Northern
Ireland
nnacht Distillery 52
The Shed Distillery 166
Ireland
Kilbeggan Distillery 114
Tullamore Distillery 168

Southwestern Ireland

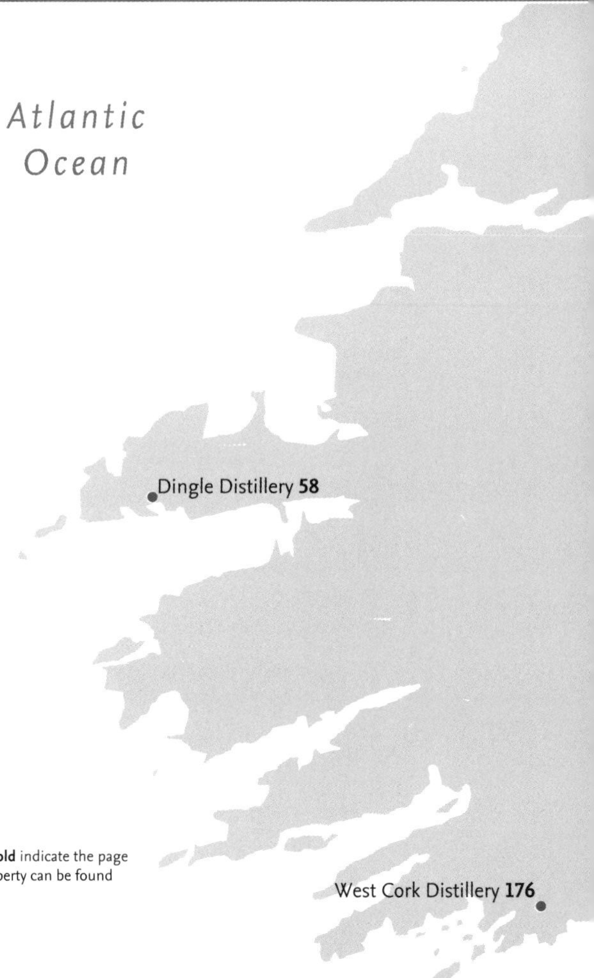

Atlantic Ocean

Dingle Distillery **58**

West Cork Distillery **176**

Numbers in **bold** indicate the page
where the property can be found

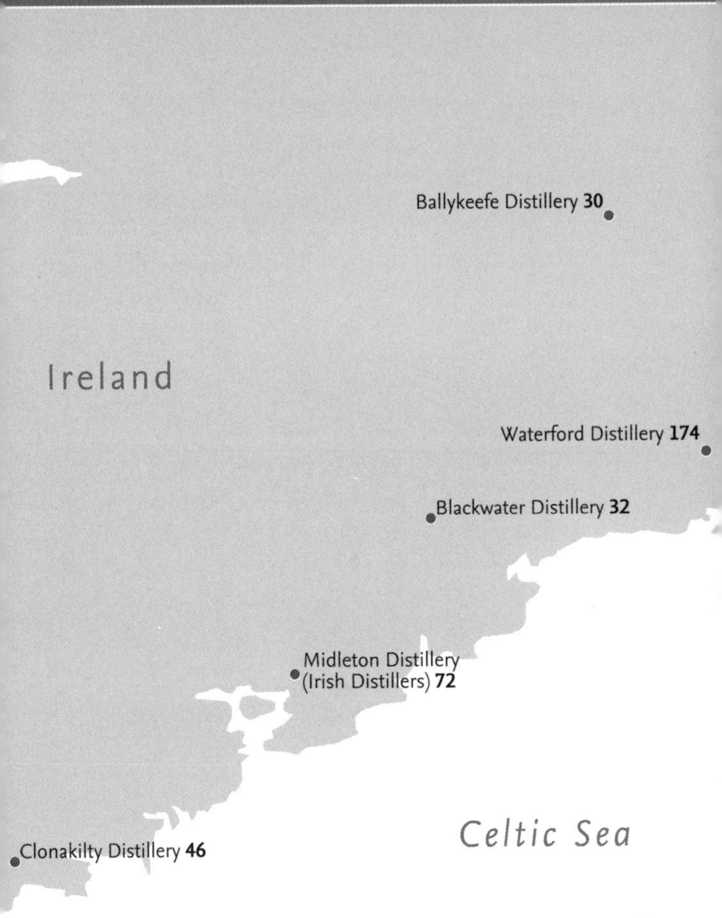

Ballykeefe Distillery **30**

Ireland

Waterford Distillery **174**

Blackwater Distillery **32**

Midleton Distillery
(Irish Distillers) **72**

Clonakilty Distillery **46**

Celtic Sea

East Central Ireland

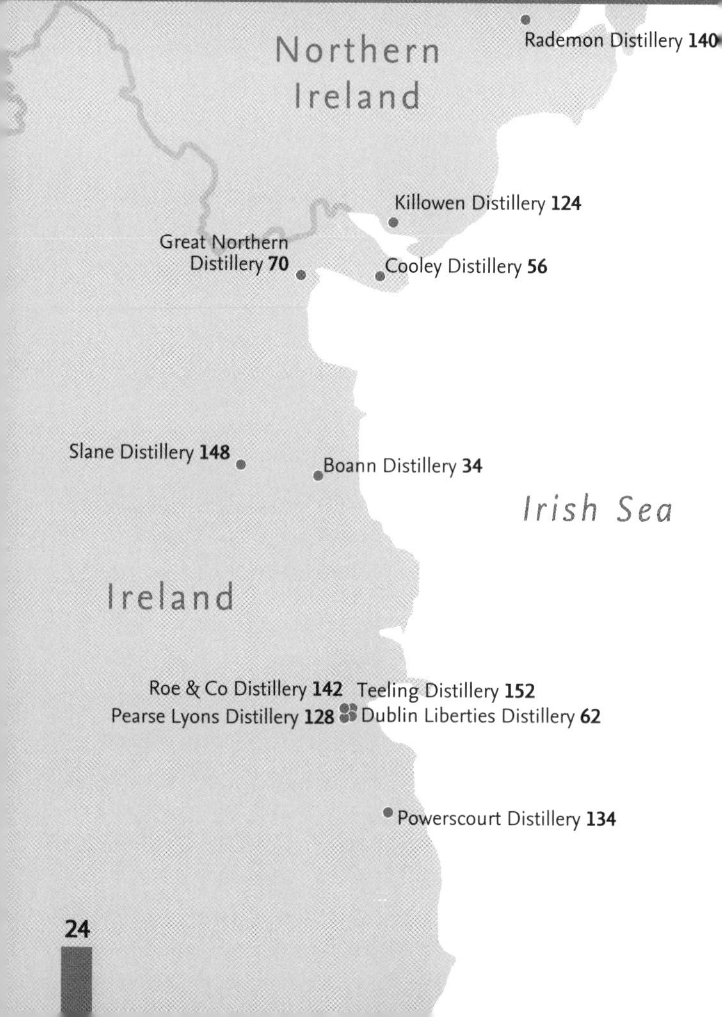
Northern Ireland
Rademon Distillery 140
Killowen Distillery 124
Great Northern Distillery 70
Cooley Distillery 56
Slane Distillery 148
Boann Distillery 34
Irish Sea
Ireland
Roe & Co Distillery 142
Teeling Distillery 152
Pearse Lyons Distillery 128
Dublin Liberties Distillery 62
Powerscourt Distillery 134

Powerscourt Distillery **134**

Irish Sea

Ireland

Royal Oak Distillery **146**

Waterford Distillery **174**

Numbers in **bold** indicate the page
where the property can be found

Celtic Sea

IRISH
WHISKEY

Achill Island Distillery

CONTACT: Drioglann Oilean Acla, Bunnacurry, Achill Island, County Mayo

WEBSITE: irishamericanwhiskeys.com

DESCRIPTION: Working distillery

A red carpet and Scottish bagpipes heralded the arrival of two copper stills on Achill Island in September 2018 from Speyside in Scotland, where they were manufactured. Drioglann Oilean Acla, as their new home is officially named in the Irish language, is the first distillery to open on an island here. It also lies within the Gaeltacht, that part of Ireland where Irish is still the first language. Owned by the Irish American Trading Company, the distillery and its visitor centre will form part of the fledgling Gaeltacht Distillery Trail, as well as being a major tourist attraction in its own right.

These days, Achill is often approached along the 42 km greenway, which links the Atlantic island to Westport in County Mayo. The greenway was built along the route of a disused railway line and is a hugely popular cycling and walking trail, which cuts through some of the most dramatic landscape in the country.

The Irish American Trading Company, a family-owned business founded by John McKay in 2014, with offices in Dublin and Boston, invested some €4 million in the project. Its master distiller, David Hynes, is also a director of the Great Northern Distillery. Currently, they use sourced whiskey to produce their two whiskeys, which are already available in twenty-six US States.

Ballykeefe Distillery

CONTACT: Ballykeefe Distillery, Kyle, Ballykeefe,
                 Cuffsgrange, County Kilkenny, R95 NR50

WEBSITE: ballykeefedistillery.ie

DESCRIPTION: Working distillery, visitor centre, and farm

There are generations of experience behind the distillery at Ballykeefe in County Kilkenny, which is built on a working beef and tillage farm. Visitors here are likely to meet farmer Morgan Ging and his wife and four children personally, as they run these two perfectly complementary businesses in the heart of rural Ireland. You are also likely to meet their cattle. The farm outhouses were converted to house their three copper stills, which were handmade in Italy by another family business, Barison Industries. The water is their own and the barley is grown on site. Maturing happens here too, in first-fill bourbon barrels, making this one of the most environmentally aware, closed-loop distilleries in the country. They simply do it all themselves.

They've already won more than thirteen international awards for their vodka, poitín, and gin, using the spirit they've distilled since 2016. Their first whiskey is due for bottling in August 2020 but their most recent sample, tasted after nineteen months in barrel, has fuelled their confidence levels. They use only the highest cut of the distillate, they say, to ensure their whiskey will be extremely smooth, and this early taste is right on target. They have a single malt, a single pot still, and a 100 per cent rye whiskey under way, as well as various blends of this trio.

Bucking the trend of other distilleries, Ballykeefe chose not to launch a sourced-whiskey brand in advance, putting all their stock in their own hard work. Despite their whiskey not being available to taste yet, there's already a well-worn route to Ballykeefe by whiskey societies and individual whiskey fans. This ambitious family affair is a really positive addition to the Irish whiskey landscape, and well worth experiencing first hand for an alternative take on who is building the category.

Blackwater Distillery

CONTACT: Blackwater Distillery, Unit 3,
                 Cappoquin Enterprise Park,
                 Cappoquin, County Waterford

WEBSITE: blackwaterdistillery.ie

DESCRIPTION: Working distillery

Blackwater Distillery have had tremendous success with their gin products, pouring huge amounts of effort into the creation of a family of gins which is trusted, innovative, and packed with personality. So, becoming the twenty-first Irish whiskey distillery to start operating here, in November 2018, sparked lots of enthusiasm for what they might conjure.

A quick glance at posts on their blog will drop you directly into a refreshing whirl of attitude and opinion on where the future of Irish whiskey is headed. They've challenged themselves in this bright new world of Irish whiskey. Experimenting with maturation isn't enough for these trailblazers to start heralding a revolution, it seems. Instead they want to create real distance between what they are creating and the rest of the field.

The people behind the distillery, founder and former broadcaster Peter Mulryan, Kieran Curtin, and the head distiller, US-born John Wilcox, feel this can only be achieved through provenance. Is their whiskey truly Irish and, if so, what determines that? The barley, the water, the wood? Blackwater will be using block-chain technology on every bottle of their double-distilled whiskey so that the customer can scan and see the full production journey, including their use of Irish grains. They'll see where exactly they mature their spirit and the kind of wood they're using. The customer will get complete transparency. That shouldn't be such a radical idea, they suggest.

They've built their business from scratch and appear to have garnered a real sense of who they are and where they want to go in doing so. They're ambitious for Irish whiskey and that's just the fuel they need.

Boann Distillery

CONTACT: Boann Whiskey Distillery, Platin Road, Drogheda, County Meath

WEBSITE: boanndistillery.ie

DESCRIPTION: Working distillery and visitor centre. Tours daily.

There aren't many distilleries in Ireland with a solid marble floor, but that was part of the luxury inheritance Boann received when they took up residence on their site in the Boyne valley, near Drogheda, on Ireland's east coast. The building that held the site before the stills arrived was a high-end car showroom and the floor laid for its cash-rich customers was too good to lose, they say. But then, the family behind this distillery are no strangers to a high-quality finish. They've been involved in the drinks industry in Ireland for decades, running the Gleeson Group before setting up Boann's parent company Na Cuana, which also has premium cider, cream liqueur, and craft beer brands in its stable.

Their beer brand bookends the distillery, and visitors to the Boann Distillery's L-shaped building can continue their journey through the Boyne Brewhouse on the same site. Boann is named after an ancient Celtic female god, who is said to have created the nearby Boyne river, which carves out this historically important slice of the Irish landscape.

They currently use sourced whiskey as their own spirit matures, but you can expect experimental collaboration with their brewhouse in future releases. Plans to use their Imperial Stout casks in finishing their whiskey are already under way. With a close eye on the environment, the Italian engineers behind their stills have included enhanced reflux control on the neck to give better control over output, they say. Additionally, they reference the use of nanotechnology in the still design, creating the conditions for much greater interaction with the copper.

The location twenty-five minutes from Dublin Airport and just off a motorway exit means that the time-poor whiskey tourist eager to get out of Dublin is going to have Boann Distillery firmly in his or her sights.

They currently source whiskey for their Whistler range and aim to produce a future range of triple-distilled single malt and single pot stills under their own steam.

The Whistler: The Blue Note

Boann created the Whistler Collection using sourced whiskey in advance of their distillery opening in 2019. Building on their contacts from their years working in the wine trade, they sourced oloroso sherry casks to age this five-year-old single malt for a further two years. Bottled at 46 per cent and non-chill filtered, it won Gold at the 2017 World Whiskey Awards. Bottled at 46 per cent.

The Whistler: 10-year-old

The 10-year-old Whistler single malt is designed to be an even smoother, more elegant take on Whistler Blue Note. Matured in ex-bourbon casks and finished in oloroso, its sweetness is strengthened by its extra time in cask. Plenty of vanilla notes, fresh summer fruit flavours, and a distinctive finish. Bottled at 46 per cent and non-chill filtered. They also produced a cask-strength version of Whistler bottled at 59 per cent.

Bushmills Distillery

CONTACT: Bushmills Distillery, 2 Distillery Road,
Bushmills, County Antrim,
Northern Ireland, BT57 8XH

WEBSITE: bushmills.com
EMAIL: visitors.bushmills@bushmills.com

DESCRIPTION: Working distillery, visitor centre,
café/bar, and shop

It's often a surprise to whiskey drinkers to find a village surrounding the famous home of Bushmills whiskey, but the more than eighty listed buildings that shape the centre of this heritage site reflect the long-held position of Bushmills as a place of industry and success.

When water was the most bankable power source around, the mill's pulling profit from the river Bush made the village a significant commercial success in this quiet corner of north Antrim, and the distillery grew from that. It's from a tributary of the same river Bush, called St Columb's Rill, that the Bushmills Distillery still takes its water today, and visitors marvel at how close they can get to a natural water source that is destined to be transformed into the core whiskeys that make up the Bushmills brand. Located just two kilometres from the dramatic Causeway Coast, the distillery receives more than 120,000 visitors a year, making it one of the most popular tourist destinations in the region.

Bushmills has changed hands many times over the centuries before current owners, Mexican liquor brand Jose Cuervos, took up residence. Its previous owner, Diageo, spent a reputed €100 million modernizing and enlarging the distillery before selling it on. Each change of ownership brought with it the promise of a continued future for the brand and the many local people who are involved in its creation. But, regardless of who has been in charge at any given time, the identity of this truly Irish and Northern Irish brand has never quite been weakened, bringing a rich and exciting layer of experience to the Irish whiskey story.

Bushmills Original

You'll find Bushmills Original in just about any bar in Ireland, its gold and white label immediately familiar among the ever more crowded shelves of Irish whiskey. It's a consistent award winner and its marriage of young grain with older, triple-distilled malt gives it a smooth creamy feel that makes it an excellent introduction to the Bushmills stable. Matured in ex-bourbon and sherry casks, you can expect vanilla and light fruit flavours. Bottled at 40 per cent.

Bushmills Red Bush

Red Bush is a recent arrival at Bushmills, having been introduced as recently as 2017. Originally aimed at the US market, it's a blend of four-year-old grain whiskey matured in first-fill bourbon casks to capture a stronger bourbon feel. It has a similar vanilla, fruit flavour to the Original, but with a sweeter finish which lingers and dominates this new entry-level whiskey. It has a darker red colour, to match its title identity. Bottled at 40 per cent.

Bushmills Black Bush

Fans of Black Bush are wholly committed to their love of this great malt and grain blend. Known by some in Ireland as "Bushmills Liquor", ordering a glass of Black Bush in a bar brings with it a hint of class that is often lacking in the identity of other Irish whiskeys. It gets its attractive dark colour from maturing in sherry casks and has a wonderful smoothness that underpins its rich, deep flavour. The blend is majority malt whiskey, aged up to 18 years. Bottled at 40 per cent.

Bushmills 10-year-old Single Malt

Triple-distilled, like all of the Bushmills family, this 100 per cent single malt is matured in bourbon and sherry casks for at least 10 years. It's a signature product in the Bushmills range and cuts to the heart of what Bushmills is famous for – rich, warm, honeyed, satisfying flavours. Chocolate and vanilla dominate and create a wonderful profile for the first of a trio of superb single malts. Bottled at 40 per cent.

Bushmills 16-year-old Single Malt

Complexity of flavour dominates this 16-year-old single malt with a layer of drama that captures all the smoothness of the 10-year-old but is stuffed full of attractive, robust added flavours. Layers of spice, honey and nuts leave a long lingering flavour. The malt is aged in both bourbon and sherry casks for around 15 years and then brought together in a port cask for up to a year, creating sweet, fruity flavours that are elegant and distinguished. Bottled at 40 per cent.

Bushmills 21-year-old Single Malt

Bushmill's top-of-the-range does not disappoint. All the rich, warm notes that define its malt heritage, underpinned by fruit, spice, nuts and toffee. It's warm and inviting and captures a sense of the indulgence that all premium whiskeys aspire to. After 19 years in oloroso sherry and bourbon casks, the two resulting single malts are combined for an additional two years in Madeira. This combination of three woods creates a delicate marriage that is very satisfying. Bottled at 40 per cent.

Clonakilty Distillery

CONTACT: Clonakilty Distillery, The Waterfront,
                Clonakilty, West Cork

WEBSITE: clonakiltydistillery.ie

DESCRIPTION: Working distillery, visitor centre,
                 and shop. Tours daily.

The family-run Clonakilty Distillery is a powerful new engine at the heart of this small County Cork town. This is a place that knows the value of a brand: it's been the home of the secret-recipe Clonakilty black pudding since the 1880s. The young distillery founded by Michael and Helen Scully is, not surprisingly, ambitious to join its famous older neighbour in the pursuit of perfectly-balanced flavours that take root in the landscape around them.

The distillery's story emerges at the point where the ocean meets the land surrounding the Galley Head lighthouse, 200 metres above the sea and a short drive from the town. It's a dramatic location, with the wind and waves of the wild Atlantic testing each generation of the Scully family that has tried to pull a living from the ground here.

The family are eighth-generation farmers, who had attempted to diversify their business a number of times before realizing the value of the barley they were growing from earth seeped in Atlantic sea salt and sand. An idea of a craft whiskey captured their imagination, and grew rapidly into a €10 million waterfront distillery in the town and a bonded warehouse on their land at the coast.

Head distiller Paul Corbett returned to his home county from his role in Teeling Distillery in Dublin to oversee operations, and distilling began in March 2019. As they wait for their own triple-distilled single pot still spirit to mature they have launched the Clonakilty brand using sourced whiskey they have blended and matured.

Clonakilty Single Batch

This award-winning blend is the first whiskey to emerge under the Clonakilty brand and was finished in its Atlantic warehouse on their land on the coast. It's a blend of eight-year-old grain and ten-year-old malt whiskey, matured in a bourbon cask, giving it that distinctive oak-derived vanilla and caramel layer. It has a spicy finish that lingers, with notes of ginger and cumin. It won Double Gold at the San Francisco Spirits Competition in 2019. Bottled at 43.6 per cent.

Clonakilty Port Cask

The Port Cask version takes the same eight-year-old grain and ten-year-old malt as the Single Batch but is finished in a port cask, giving it a spicy edge and a rich dark red colour. With no artificial colours or flavours, it is already said to be very popular in the German market. It has that Christmas pudding flavour that chocolate lovers enjoy, with lots of dark fruits and warm lingering flavours. Bottled at 43.6 per cent.

Clonakilty Single Grain Bordeaux

Clonakilty's cask series continues with this nine-year-old single grain whiskey. It's an age statement that is rare enough for a single grain. It has a rose-red colour that comes from the wine cask and is described as having flavours of red berries, custard, and sweet dessert wine. It's a light spirit with a sweet kick that lingers. Bottled at 43.6 per cent.

Connacht Whiskey Distillery

CONTACT: Connacht Whiskey Distillery, Belleek, Ballina, County Mayo, F26 P932

WEBSITE: connachtwhiskey.com

DESCRIPTION: Working distillery and gift shop. Tours run twice a day.

Connacht Whiskey Distillery sits on a bend on the river Moy in County Mayo where this famous salmon waterway finally begins to reach its destination, the Atlantic Ocean, some eight kilometres downstream. The river, the distillery, and the recently renewed woodland it neighbours, combined in recent years to rejuvenate this tranquil area – a short walk from the outskirts of Ballina. The distillery's prime location on the Wild Atlantic Way ensures tourism is big business all year round, but also helps their whiskey maturation, they say. They rely on the salty coastal scent of the river at high and low tide, as well as the scents circulating from the trees and flowers of the woodlands to filter through their casks over time, bringing that little something extra to the wood.

Still a young brand, Connacht Distillery ran its first spirit in January 2016. Time ticked by and they celebrated their first official whiskey three years and a day later, on

June 4th 2019. Master distiller Robert Cassell won't let you taste it just yet, though, as it has a few more years of maturing to do. Until then he plans to experiment with casks, finishes, and blends before releasing an aged statement single malt under the Connacht Irish Whiskey name.

The distillery was founded by a small group of American and Irish businessmen, family and friends. Apart from the Irish whiskey they are distilling, they produced a hybrid blend of American bourbon and Irish whiskey in Philadelphia called Brothership. Not quite Irish whiskey, not quite American bourbon, they see it as a celebration of journeys their families made back and forth across the Atlantic over generations.

Spade & Bushel 12

While they wait for their own spirit to mature, Connacht Distillery have created a new single malt brand using sourced whiskey, called Spade & Bushel. The first edition of this was a ten-year-old cask strength single malt which sold out. The second edition has evolved into a double-barrelled twelve-year-old single malt, bottled at 42.3 per cent. Transferring it into a new bourbon barrel and the extra two years' maturation have allowed Connacht to extend the difference between the two editions. Expect strong oaky, vanilla aromas and honeyed sweetness.

Ballyhoo Grain

Ballyhoo single grain is a four-year-old grain whiskey made with a mash blend of 93 per cent corn and 7 per cent malt whiskey. Aged in ex-bourbon and finished in port casks it's a light, entry-level whiskey that is designed for people getting to know the category better. It's a smooth, sweet whiskey with lots of dried fruit, like raisins and currants, coming from the port cask.
It has a drier taste than expected and is quite warming.
Bottled at 43 per cent.

Cooley Distillery

CONTACT: Cooley Distillery, Cooley Peninsula,
               County Louth

WEBSITE: For products see Kilbegganwhiskey.com

DESCRIPTION: Working distillery. No tours available.

The Cooley Distillery is one of two Irish distilleries owned by the international drinks giant Beam Suntory. The other is Kilbeggan in County Westmeath, which had been rebuilt by the Cooley owners before selling to Beam Suntory in 2012.

Founded by John Teeling in 1987, the establishment of the Cooley Distillery kick-started an Irish whiskey journey that has had ramifications for almost everyone in the industry here. After the huge success and subsequent sale of Cooley, John Teeling went on to found the Great Northern Distillery, which, as well as producing its own brand, supplies sourced whiskey to multiple independent whiskey bottlers and retailers, as well as other distilleries. His sons, meanwhile, created the well-known Teeling Distillery in Dublin's Liberties.

Today, Cooley distils three main brands, Connemara and the Tyrconnell, while part-production of the Kilbeggan range has moved from Cooley to the

Kilbeggan Distillery. Situated on the Cooley Peninsula in County Louth, the distillery has become chiefly a production facility since it changed ownership, with very little access to the public.

Dingle Distillery

CONTACT: Dingle Distillery, Dingle, County Kerry

WEBSITE: dingledistillery.ie

DESCRIPTION: Working distillery. Tours run four times per day. Booking essential.

The people behind Dingle Distillery were always ahead of the curve. Years before the current crop of new recruits to the Irish whiskey business, Dingle Distillery was re-inventing what it meant to be an independent craft distillery in Ireland. Three friends and business partners, Oliver Hughes, Liam la Hart, and Peter Mosley found a home for their imagination in Dingle, in County Kerry. The distillery's big blue shed across the bridge at the bottom of the town is a natural part of the landscape now, drawing praise and creating friendships all across the world. No strangers to going it alone, they are also the people behind the Porterhouse group who redrew the map for craft beer decades before it became a trend here.

Dingle has capacity to distil only a small number of casks per day, a restricted quantity that has become a virtue among its fans, encouraging sell-out releases of its four batches among a public keen to collect. The first spirit was distilled in 2012 and it created award-winning brands Dingle Gin and Dingle Vodka, while it quietly matured its single malt and pot still release.

The staff in the distillery exhibit real pride in their work, and it's hard to overestimate the difference the distillery has made to this close-knit tourist town, not just because of the employment it creates but in the shared sense of identity it conjures. It's a hard-working place, where things happen slowly and by hand: labelling, bottling, tending of casks, mashing.

A well beneath the distillery supplies the water and Dingle's microclimate, with its salty, moist Atlantic air, works its magic beneath the wood. Stories bounce around the building and tours come stuffed with personality. A visit here is a genuinely inspiring event.

Dingle Single Malt, Batch No. 4

The latest release of Dingle's single malt is the largest yet, at 30,000 bottles, aimed squarely at fulfilling international export demand. It's a triple-barrelled marriage of bourbon, sherry (Pedro Ximenez and oloroso), and port casks, which creates a great new edge for this rich and flavourful single malt. The American oak casks deliver a vanilla sweetness which combines with the dark fruits of the fortified wine casks to conjure up a taste of this Atlantic seaboard town that is entirely its own. Bottled at 46.5 per cent.

Dingle Single Pot Still, Batch No. 3

Matured exclusively in Pedro Ximenez casks, batch number two of Dingle's single pot still was a marriage of carefully selected casks. Complex and long, it has notes of dried fig and candied citrus peel, with a suggestion of warm winter spices and plum pudding. The third batch, released in late 2019 has allowed this journey to evolve, bringing an older, more complex, and sweeter pot still identity to this distinctively Kerry whiskey. Bottled at 46.5 per cent.

The Dublin Liberties Distillery

CONTACT: Dublin Liberties Distillery, 33 Mill Street,
Dublin 8, D08 V221

WEBSITE: thedld.com

DESCRIPTION: Working distillery, visitor centre,
café/bar, and shop

Not everyone will be lucky enough to have master distiller Darryl McNally show them around the DLD but, if you do, you'll get a glimpse of the passion driving this young whiskey brand. And the Derry man, who grew up in a pub before forging a career at Bushmills Distillery, will soon convince you that age truly is just a number. Although the striking cut-stone distillery at the heart of the Liberties only opened in 2019, they've immediately cast off their start-up identity. Using sourced whiskey as their own spirit matures, they are already well established in major markets around the world, courtesy of their relationship with parent group Quintessential Brands.

Already anchored to the Liberties by its 400-year-old building, the people behind the DLD went a step further by dropping a 33-metre-deep well under the building to feed its production. The building was a former tannery that processed animal skins, including the rabbit skins that were found during the DLD's €10 million renovation. It made sense then to take the brand name Dead Rabbit, which the group already owned, referencing the notorious New York-based Irish immigrant gang of the same name, and partner with their friends at the Dead Rabbit bar in Manhattan to produce the Dead Rabbit whiskey.

On the first floor of the DLD is a beautifully finished bar that runs the length of the building and overlooks their three copper stills. It's undoubtedly the best place to discover their story.

The Dubliner range

The Dubliner is the DLD entry point and is described as their answer to Jameson and Tullamore D.E.W. It's an incredibly versatile whiskey, allowing DLD to produce a range of variants that includes the three-year-old green label, the master distiller's blue label, a white-labelled Tannery exclusive, and a ten-year-old single malt. It's also the base for their best-selling honeycomb-flavoured Dubliner Liqueur, while a recent collaboration with local brewers Rascals produced a limited-edition beer cask series, introducing flavours like smoked stout and vanilla and cinnamon. Dubliner ten-year-old is bottled at 42 per cent.

Dublin Liberties Oak Devil

The Oak Devil takes its name from the carving that was on entry points to the Liberties, warning them of the type of area they were entering. DLD use it to signal the entry point of their premium and prestige range. This whiskey is a five-year-old blend which puts it in a slightly premium position, as there are few blends of this age produced. It's matured in bourbon casks and non-chill filtered like all of DLD's range, so expect smooth flavours of vanilla, wood, and spice. Bottled at 46 per cent.

Dublin Liberties Copper Alley

This ten-year-old single malt is limited specifically by the quality of its finish. Master distiller Darryl McNally personally obtained thirty-year-old oloroso sherry casks for Copper Alley in Spain, but could only get thirty-one of them, so, unless the cask stock is replenished, it will be rarely repeated. A double gold winner at the International Wine and Spirits Awards, Copper Alley spent ten years in bourbon before its Spanish finish. Rich flavours of chocolate and dark fruit with a nutty finish. Bottled at 46 per cent.

Dublin Liberties Murder Lane

This thirteen-year-old triple-distilled single malt is the first of Dublin Liberties' three prestige expressions. Matured in bourbon and then finished in Hungarian Tokay casks. Tokay is a dessert wine, and so it brings rich sweet flavours like coconut, bananas, and apple to this single malt. The goal was to create a single malt that would bring edge, depth, and character, and that would set it apart within the DLD range. Murder Lane was an infamous alleyway in the Liberties, where it's claimed many people lost their lives. Bottled at 46 per cent.

Dublin Liberties Keepers Coin

Keepers Coin is a superbly rich sixteen-year-old single malt that will linger long after it has been tasted. Every one of the sixteen years can be tasted in this smooth, full-flavoured whiskey. It truly is remarkable. Matured in first-fill bourbon casks, it is finished in Pedro Ximenez sherry casks, delivering a rich honey sweetness that is both surprising and long. Bottled at 46 per cent.

Dublin Liberties King of Hell

Hand-bottled and with a €2,700 price tag that puts it at the ultra-premium end of the market, this 27-year-old single malt is rightly the king of the range. Master distiller Darryl McNally feels that anything aged over twenty years starts to pick up very woody, spicy notes. To counter this, once the whiskey was sourced, he matured it further in a Bordeaux Premier Cru wine cask, allowing this extra finish to bring out a really balanced flavour that he describes as "to die for". With only fifty bottles produced in the initial batch, McNally plans to continue with more prestige aged variants. Bottled at 46 per cent.

Great Northern Distillery

CONTACT: Great Northern Distillery, Carrick Road, Dundalk, County Louth

WEBSITE: gndireland.com

DESCRIPTION: Working distillery

The Great Northern Distillery (GND) in Dundalk is aptly named. It's a huge operation, and the largest independent distillery in Ireland. Created by John Teeling and his partners after the sale of the Cooley and Kilbeggan Distilleries to Beam Suntory, it is part of a relatively new economy built around contract distilling in bulk for other distilleries and third parties. This could include, for example, small distilleries that haven't yet matured their own spirit, it could be as a supplement to existing mature spirit, or it could be the whiskey source of independent brands that are bonding and blending their own whiskey, but not distilling.

Throughout this book, distilleries will be referenced as using sourced whiskey. GND is one of only a very small number of distilleries with the capacity to be that source. It was set up in a former Diageo brewery that latterly brewed Harp Lager in the town of Dundalk. Its first three-year-old whiskey came of age in 2018.

Using water from the Cooley peninsula, it produces grain whiskey, triple-distilled malt whiskey, double-distilled malt whiskey, peated malt whiskey, and pot still whiskey. Its output is phenomenal – it has a current capacity of sixteen million litres of whiskey spirit. It also produces a poitín and a gin.

In addition to its bulk whiskey, in 2018 it launched an own-label whiskey called Burke's, a fifteen-year-old single cask bottled at 57.5 per cent, or natural cask strength.

As Great Northern Distillery is a large-scale production facility, it doesn't run tours.

Irish Distillers

CONTACT: Irish Distillers, Head Office,
              Simmonscourt, Ballsbridge, Dublin

WEBSITE: irishdistillers.ie

DESCRIPTION: Working distillery

Irish Distillers is one part of the global drinks giant Pernod Ricard. It was first created in the late 1960s, in what many feared was the end game for Irish whiskey distilling. The industry was in severe decline, prompted by economic, political, and cultural shifts that impacted all areas of Irish industry, but whiskey in particular. Independent distilleries all around the country were falling silent and, in an act of self-preservation, three major distilleries merged.

The people behind the merger hoped that by combining their strengths they could forge a new future for their brands. The distilleries were Cork Distilleries Company, and the two Dublin distilleries, John Jameson and Son, and Powers and Son. (In 1972 Bushmills also joined Irish Distillers before being sold to Diageo in 2005.)

Neither of the two Dublin distilleries offered the space needed to create a new distillery that could handle the output of all three, so the decision was made to close the Dublin distilleries (Jameson at Bow Street and Powers at John's Lane) and move all their production to Midleton in Cork. The new Midleton Distillery opened in 1975 and thrives today.

Irish Distillers is now the biggest distiller of Irish whiskey in the country, managing six major whiskey brands, each with a global outlook: Jameson, Powers, Redbreast, Method and Madness, Midleton VR, and the Spot range.

Jameson Irish Whiskey

CONTACT: Irish Distillers, Midleton Distillery, Cork; and Bow Street, Dublin

WEBSITE: jamesonwhiskey.com

DESCRIPTION: Working distillery, visitor centre and shop

Even though I had heard all about the roaring success of Jameson in the US, it was only when I stood at the bar of a Chicago blues club a decade ago and watched a steady stream of young American music fans order round after round of this classic Irish whiskey that the true impact of Irish distillers' work sank in. It was a strange sensation to witness a brand that I felt was so local, and even ordinary, be embraced by an audience as hip and international as the random sample I was experiencing. But such is the power of Jameson. It is by far the best-selling Irish whiskey globally, with sales reaching over seven million cases in 2018.

Of course, Jameson is no stranger to the USA. It has been on the international market since the nineteenth century. It's also a whiskey with great lineage. It was founded in 1780 by a Scotsman, John Jameson, who with his wife Margaret Haig (the daughter of John Haig, another famous Scottish distiller) had sixteen children.

It is not surprising, then, to see Jameson have almost as many variants in its own whiskey family since.

Now part of the Irish Distillers group, Jameson is distilled in the Midleton Distillery in Cork, a twenty-four-hour, seven days a week operation that can hardly pause for breath, such is the growth in demand. The old Jameson Distillery at Bow Street in Dublin is now a state-of-the art museum so, if you can't make it to Cork, you can still enjoy the full experience in the capital.

Jameson Original

The original Jameson is a blend of single pot still whiskey and grain whiskey, triple-distilled and aged for four years in bourbon casks to give it the fine balance of spice, vanilla, and sherry that has become its trademark. It's a smooth, well-rounded whiskey with legions of fans around the world. Bottled at 40 per cent.

Jameson Crested

Previously known as Crested 10, this was always a popular variant of Jameson in rural Irish bars. After a design revamp in 2016, the 10 in its name was dropped to simplify the name – the 10 was not related to the age of the whiskey. The simpler title suits this blend of single pot still and grain whiskey, and the richer flavours of sherry and honey in this step away from Jameson Original gives it its own identity. Bottled at 40 per cent.

Jameson Caskmates

This great two-part series is a marriage of craft beer and whiskey distilling. Starting with a stout edition, Jameson collaborated with Franciscan Well brewery in Cork to see what a barrel used to make stout would do to Jameson. It was a big success, delivering notes of chocolate, coffee, and butterscotch. They followed this with an IPA edition, to conjure a much lighter, herbal, fruit layer. Bottled at 40 per cent.

Jameson Black Barrel

Traditionally, casks are burned or charred on the inside by coopers before they are filled with whiskey to re-invigorate the chemical reactions that are stimulated between the wood and the whiskey. The casks used for Black Barrel get a double charring, which is designed to amplify this effect. It's a blend of grain and single pot still whiskeys, which pulls a nuttier, deeper flavour from the char, as well as stronger vanilla flavours. Bottled at 40 per cent.

Jameson Makers Series

This series was created to reference the craftspeople behind the whiskey – coopers, distillers, and blenders. There are three whiskeys in the range. Distiller's Safe by head distiller Brian Nation is a blend of pot still and grain, which celebrates the pot still element in particular. The Cooper's Croze by Ger Buckley is all about wood, according to Irish Distillers, as it is aged in a variety of woods. Blender's Dog by head blender Billy Leighton is all about balance, they say. (A dog is the cup a blender uses to take samples from a cask.) Each is bottled at 43 per cent.

Jameson 18-year-old Bow St. Edition

This 18-year-old premium whiskey is a marriage of three distillates and is matured in both bourbon and sherry before a final finish in fresh bourbon barrels. The Bow Street edition is said to be the rarest in the Jameson family and is considered very mellow and smooth. Expect toffee, oak, vanilla, and sherry nuttiness. It's a high-end finish and is bottled just once a year at cask strength.

Powers

CONTACT: Irish Distillers

WEBSITE: powerswhiskey.com

DESCRIPTION: Working distillery

If you're ever lucky enough to get into the Powers archive at their Midleton Distillery in Cork, you'll discover centuries of records charting the global success of this great Irish brand. Powers whiskey conquered the world in its lifetime, remaining at the centre of the international Irish whiskey story during its rise, fall, and current re-invention. But every story you hear, whether about its new Cork home, its success around the globe, or the pot still flavours at its heart, will eventually cast your imagination back to Dublin, where it all began.

Powers remains knitted into the fabric of the capital. You'll be startled at the sight of the original stills in what is now the National College of Art and Design (pictured), or realizing the underground car park on Drury Street is the former bottling hall, where (mostly) women worked, packaging and distributing the brand around the world. In the Victorian pubs of Dublin you'll find antique gold-leaf adorned Powers mirrors that have reflected Dublin life for over two hundred years. And, in a bizarre twist, the Powers founder James Power, buried in 1817 in St James Graveyard on Thomas Street, has been knitted once again into the Irish whiskey story: the church building that casts a shadow across his grave has been converted into one of Dublin's youngest whiskey distilleries, the Pearse Lyons Distillery.

The people driving Powers today, under Irish Distillers and Pernod Ricard, recognize the value of this heritage and recently established the Powers Quarter in Dublin, essentially creating a district that is defined by Powers landmarks and a selection of Dublin bars that they hope can bring you to the heart of the brand.

Powers Gold Label

You'll find Powers Gold Label in almost
every bar in Ireland. It's a blend of
largely pot still and a smaller amount
of grain whiskey that has a distinctive
peppery taste. Once the best-selling
Irish whiskey, its smooth, sweet
flavours continue to be hugely
popular. It offers a layer of
sophistication in its flavour profile
that is rarely found in a whiskey
at this price level. Aged in
American oak casks, it has a
spicy, honeyed finish that
lingers. Bottled at 40 per cent.

Powers Three Swallows

When devising the Three Swallows release, Irish Distillers set out to create a modern take on the original Powers recipe. They wanted something that would be wholly pot still but have an edge that reflected how far the whiskey brand has come. It doesn't have an age statement but Three Swallows is a strong, spicy whiskey, matured in ex-bourbon barrels and married with a small amount of sherry-aged whiskey. This bourbon/sherry combination gives it a richer, silkier feel than Gold Label. Bottled at 40 per cent.

Powers Signature Release

Reportedly set to be discontinued (making it an automatic collector's item), this sometimes overlooked member of the Powers family was the second single pot still to be added to the family after John's Lane. Powers Signature Release comes packed with all the spicy notes that Powers fans expect. Matured in bourbon, it contains a small amount of whiskey matured in oloroso. Bottled at 46 per cent.

Powers John's Lane

This Single Pot Still was a return to the heart of Powers and its original, earthy recipe. Using whiskey aged for at least twelve years, they set out to create a whiskey that was worthy of taking the name of their original distillery at John's Lane. It doesn't disappoint, and John's Lane is rightly celebrated as the ultra-premium Powers release. With lingering flavours of spice, vanilla, dark fruit, and honey, it is unmistakably Powers, with a strong oaky finish. Bottled at 46 per cent.

Redbreast

CONTACT: Irish Distillers

WEBSITE: redbreastwhiskey.com

DESCRIPTION: Working distillery

Redbreast is a champion of Irish whiskey. With five siblings, this is a family of considerable distinction that has won almost every whiskey accolade in the world. The twelve-year-old Redbreast is the world's biggest-selling single pot still Irish whiskey.

It's the bedrock for a brand on continuous sale since 1912, when the then maker, W&A Gilbey of London, decided to name its various Dublin-made pot still whiskeys after birds – reportedly prompted by his membership of the Royal Ornithological Society. By the 1980s Gilbey's was struggling and pot still whiskey was deeply out of fashion. Irish Distillers bought the label in 1984 but didn't start producing their own Redbreast until 1991.

Irish whiskey fans are largely united in their respect for the brand, holding it in an almost romantic position in their minds. This is helped by the fact that this is a whiskey brand that somehow conjures up a sense of winter, or even Christmas, with roaring fires, crackling logs, and long, dark nights. While newer variants on the original twelve-year-old have helped differentiate the brand from the colder months, it is still celebrated by Irish Distillers as something that anchors the winter season, with Christmas cake often heralded as a signature flavour in the signature twelve-year-old.

The combination of malted and unmalted barley in this single pot still creates the peppery, creamy sensation that defines Redbreast. Triple-distilled, it's matured in American oak from Kentucky and Tennessee and oloroso sherry barrels from Jerez in Spain. Incredibly smooth, it's recommended that you drink it neat.

The latest adventure in the Redbreast range is Redbreast Dream Cask, a very limited-edition release of thirty-two-year-old single pot still that really took the world by storm. There was an immediate sell-out of both editions.

Redbreast 12

The leader of the pack, this twelve-year-old single pot still has everything going for it. The original source of the Christmas cake flavour description, it is packed with surprises, not least its unmistakable single pot still identity. For many, it's the first discovery of the combined creamy, peppery, fruity flavours and textures that make Redbreast spark such devotion in fans. There is nothing about Redbreast that emulates other brands. It's a singular experience that rarely disappoints. Bottled at 40 per cent.

Redbreast Lustau

Redbreast Lustau is a wonderful marriage of Irish Distillers' Redbreast and the Bodegas Lustau in Jerez, Spain. Lustau is considered the premier sherry producer in that part of the Iberian peninsula. Hugely popular with Redbreast fans, it is matured for nine to twelve years in Spanish oak with a final year in an oloroso cask. Oak dominates, but also the gingerbread character of the Lustau, when combined with the spice of the single pot still creates a rich ginger finish. Bottled at 46 per cent.

Redbreast 15

The fifteen-year-old Redbreast first appeared in 2005 and its popularity made sure it became a permanent member of the team. It can contain whiskey aged from fifteen to nineteen years. The extra time in cask is designed to create a fuller body and deeper wood undertones. The wood certainly is dominant but it also delivers sweet and spicy fruit flavours. Like the entire Redbreast family, there's a smooth creaminess to the fifteen-year-old, with a rich, decadent finish. Bottled at 46 per cent.

Redbreast 21

This is the ultra-premium end of the Redbreast line and it has no end of dedicated fans. It's rich and full and is a stunning example of single pot still. The peppery spices and the rich fruit flavours so well conjured during its twenty-one years maturing in oloroso and sherry casks make this a whiskey for marking the most special of occasions. Complex and surprising, it has a wonderful finish that remains long after the last drop. Superb depth and flavour. Bottled at 46 per cent.

Method and Madness

CONTACT: Irish Distillers

WEBSITE: methodandmadnesswhiskey.com

DESCRIPTION: Working distillery

Establishing a microdistillery at the heart of Ireland's largest distillery was an unexpected move for an operation so in demand that it rarely stops production. Its output, the Midleton Distillery's youngest brand, Method and Madness, was in fact launched as a quartet: a Single Grain, a Single Malt, a Single Pot Still, and a thirty-one-year-old Single Cask, Single Grain whiskey. Additional products have been added since. There's no room in the whiskey business for regret, it seems, so they've created something for everyone.

Irish Distillers know better than most what the success of Jameson did for the Irish whiskey market internationally. As satisfying as it is to see millions of litres of whiskey production flow through their distillery each year, master distiller Brian Nation knows that, for customers, graduating from Jameson can't be about simply picking the next bottle from the shelf. He and his team plan to keep that graduate buyer firmly in the family and while their niche connoisseur brands, like Redbreast, the Spot range, and Midleton Very Rare, do a great job at that, he says, getting the opportunity to create a whole new range at a price point that's accessible is crucial.

The method and the madness in its name references the distillery's masters and apprentices who collaborated on the range, using expert knowledge to drive fresh new ideas while also training a whole new generation of distillers, blenders, and coopers. It's a strong angle to forge a new brand and its core range plus special limited edition casks have caught the attention of both new young drinkers and seasoned fans looking for something new.

Method and Madness Single Grain

The entry-level expression in the Method and Madness range is the single grain. At launch it was the first official release of a single grain from Midleton and the first dive into experimentation in this range. Matured in bourbon barrels and finished in virgin Spanish oak, it has a subtle aroma and a stronger more vanilla flavour and long finish. A gold medal winner at the Irish Whiskey Awards in 2017 and 2018 for Best Irish Single Grain. Bottled at 46 per cent.

Method and Madness Single Malt

Single malts are a rare occurrence at Midleton so this non-age statement bottling came with high expectations. Judging from the great reception from customers, they were well met. The spirit was reportedly laid down in 2002 in ex-bourbon barrels and then part-finished in French oak. It's a wonderful example of single malt, with beautiful light aromas and rich biscuit, vanilla, and cinnamon flavours. With no added colouring, it's carved a very particular niche in this already experimental range. Bottled at 46 per cent.

Method and Madness Single Pot Still

This rich spicy single pot still spent nine years in a combination of sherry and bourbon casks before being finished for a year in French Chestnut casks. At the time of launch the use of chestnut was extremely rare. It's the same family as oak and beech but a porous wood with an open grain that matures the spirit faster. The result was a single pot still that comes stuffed with a fresh deep flavour, with that distinctive spicy finish of single pot still. Lots of fruit, honey, cream, and cinnamon. Bottled at 46 per cent. For a very special alternative, look for their limited edition Virgin Hungarian Oak Finish Single Pot Still.

Method and Madness
31-year-old Single Grain

This thirty-one-year-old spirit, which has been ageing quietly in the deep recesses of Midleton's warehouses, has finally found its purpose. Emerging after all these years from an ex-bourbon cask, the flavour is suitably dark, rich, and sweet. Packed with flavour and personality, the expression is made up of three single casks but, although discontinued, it has a price point significant enough to ensure it won't get snapped up too quickly. One for the collectors. Bottled at 51.8 per cent.

Method and Madness Single Pot Still finished in Wild Cherry Wood

Cherry wood is common across Europe and is more frequently crafted into musical instruments than whiskey casks, but this diversion is a wonderful use of this romantic, flavourful wood. This world's first single pot still is a superb example of what experimental thinking can deliver. The porous nature of cherry wood allows much greater interaction between the whiskey and the wood, delivering an intense pocket of flavour. The naturally dark colour and prickly, spicy finish is immediately attractive, long-lasting, and rich. Expect layers of coconut, ginger, and green herbs, with toasted hazelnut. This is something very special. Bottled at 46 per cent.

Method and Madness Single Pot Still finished in Acacia Wood

Using the very same spirit base as the cherry wood variant, the team driving this exciting range has conjured up a completely different whiskey by using different wood. Acacia wood seeks out dry, shallow soil, its small white flowers blooming in spring. The wood is less porous than cherry, its slower interaction delivering a chocolaty, nutty flavour and a darker, mahogany colour. Indeed, everything tastes darker in this wonderful pot still – dark fruits, coffee beans, crushed cloves. It's rich, long-lasting, and a quick friend. Bottled at 46 per cent.

Midleton VR

CONTACT: Irish Distillers

WEBSITE: midletonveryrare.com

DESCRIPTION: Working distillery

There's a room in the picture-perfect distiller's cottage at the heart of the Midleton Distillery that has every bottle of Midleton Very Rare since it began life in 1984. Looking at that first bottle now, and having lived in Ireland that year, I'm prompted to ask one question: who would be mad enough to create a luxury brand in the depths of one of Ireland's worst recessions? The man, of course, was not at all mad, but visionary, and his name was Barry Crockett.

Born in the distiller's cottage, Crockett grew up to be a master distiller like his father. Just a few short years after Irish Distillers took up residence at Midleton, he set about creating what he intended would be the very best whiskey he had ever made – Midleton VR. The result is superb.

It's highly collectable, and older bottles are wonderfully expensive, with each year's bottle gaining value as the new one is introduced. Buy that year's edition, however, and it's not at all overpriced, currently at around €180 a bottle in Ireland. Each edition produces around 2,500 bottles per year of whiskey that is hand-selected from the distillery's warehouses. Each vintage is different and each bottle is individually numbered and signed by Barry Crockett or his successor Brian Nation, who is now head distiller.

It is an incredible luxury to sit in the distiller's cottage and sample this range. Not only does the house transport you to another time, the Midleton VR will conjure an experience in flavour that is simply outstanding. Conversation will inevitably flow to whether great whiskey should be collected or consumed. I vote to drink every time, just to be rich in the moment.

Midleton Vintage Release 2018

Each year since 1984, a single vintage of Midleton VR has been produced, in recent years usually numbering 2,500 bottles. The whiskey in the 2018 vintage was hand-selected by Brian Nation and blended to create his very personal imagining of that year's Midleton VR. A deeply complex whiskey, it has incredible flavour, with a wonderful creamy texture, layered with vanilla, oak, apple, and pepper. A long, luxurious finish. Bottled at 40 per cent.

Barry Crockett Legacy

Remarkably, the Midleton Barry Crockett Legacy is the first Irish Distillers product to be named after a master distiller since John Jameson. It was created as a permanent single pot still in 2011 to mark the impact this man has had on the output of Midleton and on Irish Distillers. It's an incredibly elegant whiskey, with dark pepper, citrus, rich vanilla, and oak. Stuffed full of flavour, it has a wonderful finish. Bottled at 46 per cent.

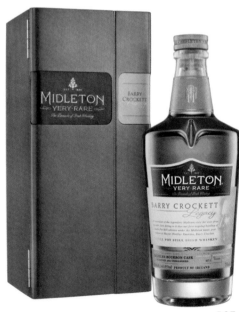

Midleton VR Dair Ghaelach Grinsell's Wood

To understand how incredibly rare this whiskey is, you need to realize how little Irish oak there is left in Ireland. For Dair Ghaelach Grinsell's Wood, nine 130-year-old oak trees were used to source the oak to make the barrels. The effect of the Irish oak on the distillate was unknown in advance but conjured a whiskey of superior sophistication and deep flavour: chocolate, vanilla, pepper, spice, and fudge, with a beautifully long finish that travels. Bottled at 58.2 per cent.

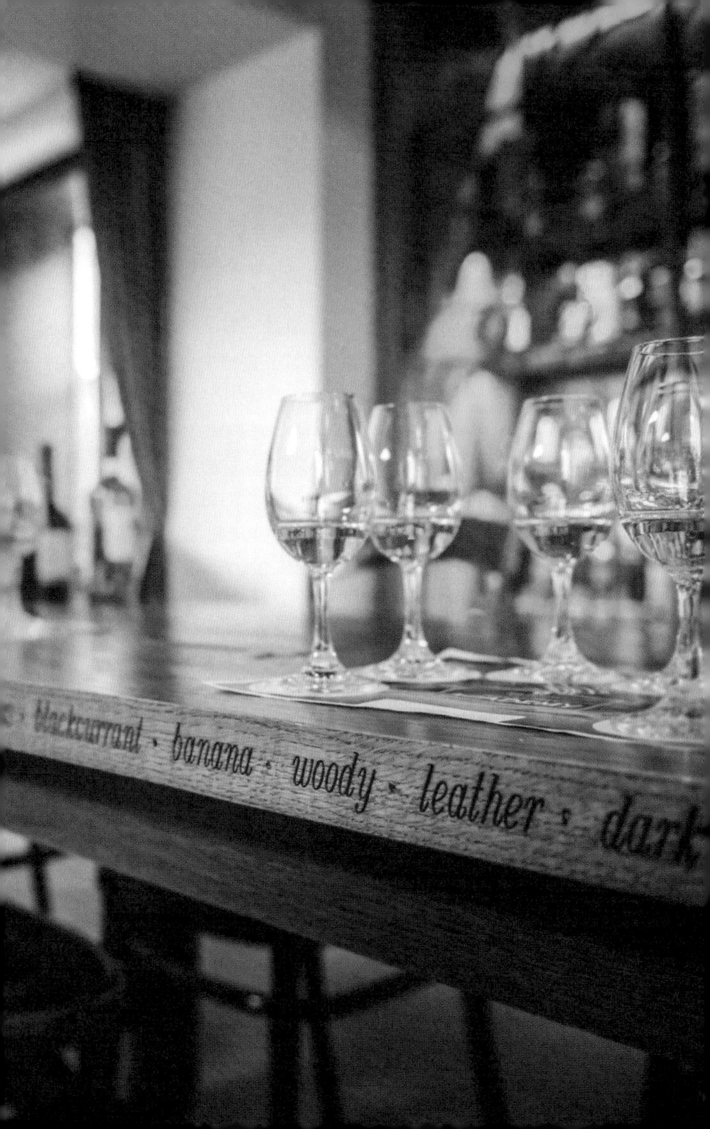
blackcurrant • banana • woody • leather • dark

The Spot range

CONTACT: Irish Distillers

WEBSITE: spotwhiskey.com

DESCRIPTION: Working distillery

Green Spot, Yellow Spot, Red Spot – this single pot still range is the brand that just keeps giving. Since it was first created in the cellars of Mitchell & Son in the late 1800s, what is now known as the Spot range won legions of fans. It was a simpler time, when the noble art of blending and bonding whiskey was just part of the whiskey landscape. Mitchell & Son were wine and spirit merchants, who used sherry and port casks they had imported to fashion a whole new flavour profile, using Jameson sourced from the then working distillery of Bow Street. The spots and their respective colours came from the Mitchell family's habit of marking casks of different ages – Blue for seven years, Green for ten years, Yellow for twelve years, and Red for fifteen years.

More than a century later, the whiskey is just as celebrated. Still created for Mitchell & Son, it is distilled and matured in Midleton Distillery in Cork as part of Irish Distillers. Rich and spicy, each pot still is a different age and recipe. Blue spot remains waiting in the wings to be revived but the other three colours are each back on the shelves. Red Spot re-emerged to great fanfare last year and immediately sold out. Green Spot, which is the only one that has been continuously distilled since the beginning, has two additional variants, forging even more meaningful connections.

Green Spot

Always limited, this gentle spicy whiskey is the only uninterrupted brand from the various spot colours, and is incredibly popular. Now a non-age statement whiskey, it is based on the original ten-year-old recipe of the traditional pot still Green Spot, but with whiskey of between seven and ten years of age. Light and smooth, it has tons of personality and comes stuffed with fruit, vanilla and warm honey flavours. Bottled at 40 per cent.

Yellow Spot

This twelve-year-old single pot still
has been matured in bourbon, sherry,
and Pedro Ximenez wine casks,
giving it a wonderfully mature and
complex identity. A multiple award
winner, the pot still comes laced
with honey, citrus, and deep vanilla,
with a characteristic spiced finish
and a delicious sweetness.
Bottled at 46 per cent.

Red Spot

The revival of fifteen-year-old
Red Spot was a triumph. A quick
sell-out in its first batch, the
triple-distilled single pot still was
matured in a combination of casks
pre-seasoned with bourbon,
oloroso sherry, and Marsala
fortified wine. Expect flavours of
rich dark fruit, elegant honeyed
layers, and bursts of spice and
pepper. Bottled at 46 per cent.

Green Spot: the variations

Careful connections have produced very special Green Spot variations. The first to emerge was a relationship with Chateau Leoville Barton, a vineyard established by another old Irish family, whose wine casks were used to finish this special edition. Following that, a US partnership was born when Green Spot was finished for twelve months in French oak Zinfandel from Chateau Montelena in Napa Valley in California. Both bottled at 46 per cent.

Kilbeggan Distillery

CONTACT: Kilbeggan Distillery, Lower Main Street, Aghamore, Kilbeggan, County Westmeath

WEBSITE: kilbegganwhiskey.com

DESCRIPTION: Working distillery, visitor centre, and shop

A distillery was founded on the Kilbeggan site in this County Westmeath town in 1757. Previously known as Locke's, it's Ireland's oldest but, like so many others, it closed its doors in the 1950s in the face of economic difficulty. Bought and restored by the people behind the Cooley Distillery, it now serves as the public face of Japanese drinks giant Beam Suntory's operations in Ireland. Beam Suntory bought the Cooley and Kilbeggan distilleries in 2012.

Cooley now does the majority of the distilling for their three brands, Kilbeggan, Connemara, and Tyrconnell whiskeys. The Kilbeggan Distillery produces its own rye whiskey in its two pot stills just off the distillery courtyard, and matures spirit from Cooley for the Kilbeggan range in its warehouses.

It's a fascinating place to visit, offering one of the clearest experiences of what a working distillery would have been like at the height of the Irish whiskey boom. Before it was bought, local people had taken it upon themselves to save the building and the great water wheel that drives the mill was central to their plan to bring this historic building at the heart of the town back to life. On a tour you're brought through the building and you get to see the water wheel and the then cutting-edge machinery that it powered. It's a powerful testament to naturally derived power. But, perhaps more importantly, what the local people saved and Cooley restored is a wonderful record of the simplicity of whiskey production.

Kilbeggan Irish Whiskey

This title brand for the range is a double-distilled blend of malt and grain whiskey. Matured in bourbon casks, it is produced at Kilbeggan's sister distillery, Cooley. It's a light, easy-drinking whiskey which its makers suggest is a good cocktail base, as well as for drinking neat. Expect light fruit flavours with a hint of malt biscuit. Short enough finish. Pale gold in colour. Bottled at 40 per cent.

Kilbeggan Small Batch Rye

In the courtyard of the Kilbeggan Distillery are two very attractive small copper pot stills, one of which is the oldest working copper pot still in Ireland. The spirit distilled here is used to make this new small batch rye whiskey. It's the first whiskey to be fully distilled and matured on site since the distillery was re-opened. Rye is relatively rare in Irish whiskey and the heritage recipe used calls for 30 per cent rye. Expect a spiciness, coupled with a warm vanilla and malt biscuit. It has a long buttery finish. Bottled at 43 per cent.

Kilbeggan Single Grain

There's 6 per cent malt and 94 per cent corn in the mash bill for Kilbeggan's single grain. Aged in ex-bourbon barrels and fortified wine barrels, it has a smooth, sweet, and nutty flavour, with a short finish of fruit and spice. It was the winner of Best Irish Single Grain at the 2018 Irish Whiskey Awards. Bottled at 43 per cent.

Connemara Original Peated Single Malt

This peated single malt is a rare treat for fans of smoky whiskey in the Irish market. Produced at Cooley, the peated malt comes from Scotland and would have been a much more common flavour profile in Ireland back in the eighteenth century, when barley was dried over fires, often fuelled by peat. Combined with Cooley's distinctive double-distilled sweet malt layers, it's a distinctive brand that delivers lots of flavour. Bottled at 40 per cent.

Connemara 12-year-old Single Malt

The twelve-year-old version of this peated single malt is a robust, flavourful whiskey. Everything feels more tightly packed with the extra maturation, and fruit, vanilla, and spiced ginger coming through alongside herbs and black pepper. The smoke isn't intense but is richly combined with the single malt, and there's a long finish that is nicely balanced with the peat. Bottled at 40 per cent.

Tyrconnell Single Malt

This is the signature single malt in the Tyrconnell range. A much-loved whiskey among Cooley fans, the double-distilled spirit is aged in bourbon and comes packed with summer fruits and tropical notes, with a long spicy finish. The Tyrconnell was the name of a racehorse that captured the imagination of a whiskey maker in 1876 who created the first Tyrconnell whiskey. It is said to have been a surprise success. Cooley revived the brand and the Tyrconnell success continues. Bottled at 43 per cent.

Tyrconnell Cask Series

The Tyrconnell Cask Series is a series of three 10-year-old single malts, which spend nine years maturing in bourbon barrels before finishing for a further six to eight months in one of three casks – sherry, port, or Madeira – before being returned to bourbon. Each of the finishes in the series creates a rich and decadent flavour profile. Although it was originally created as a limited edition, its popularity made it a permanent part of the range. Bottled at 46 per cent.

Tyrconnell 16-year-old Single Malt

The Tyrconnell 16 won double gold at the San Francisco World Spirits competition in 2017. A really superb addition to the Tyrconnell family, it spent fifteen years in bourbon, before finishing for a further period in a Madeira wine cask. It's rich and full of flavour, with an elegant feel. Expect lots of dark fruit and fresh spice, with a long peppery finish with a citrus edge. A very popular step up in the range for Tyrconnell fans. Bottled at 46 per cent.

Killowen Distillery

CONTACT: Killowen Distillery, 29 Kilfeaghan Road, Killowen, County Down, Northern Ireland, BT34 3AW

WEBSITE: killowendistillery.com

DESCRIPTION: Microdistillery and visitor centre

Brendan Carty, the young architect and distiller who has put all his ambition into this tiny distillery up a remote mountain lane in County Down, is on a remarkable journey. He's taken an old stables building and reshaped everything by hand – the roof, the floor, the insulation, and the corner bar, where visitors sit to taste his gin, poitín, and, eventually, the whiskey he's maturing. From the front door to the back wall is a mere ten metres, but in that distance you'll travel through time as you experience Carty's take on creating a new Irish whiskey brand.

It's a place stuffed with ideas and driving it all are two beautiful copper stills that Carty heats by flame, a laborious undertaking that demands all his skill and attention. These are coupled with two worm tub condensers, which, he believes, makes Killowen the only distillery in Ireland that relies on the worm tub approach alone.

His whiskey is quietly maturing in Pedro Ximenez sherry casks. In April 2019 he laid down the first cask of a smoked single pot still whiskey, using a historic mash bill that involved lots of green barley and oats, wheat, and malted barley. The malted barley is smoked in a hand-built kiln fuelled by turf from the majestic Mourne Mountains around him. The water is pulled from this dramatic place too, ensuring the entire operation is rooted in the land upon which it stands. His family are also rooted in this place, as well as in the counties of Donegal and Antrim, where they run two well-known pubs.

Everything about this place is authentic — even the image of the megalithic tomb he puts on his label (the Kilfeaghan Dolmen) can be found standing on the land near the distillery, where it has weathered storms for centuries. Here's hoping Killowen's stills will stand alongside it for an equally long time too.

Lough Measc Distillery

CONTACT: Lough Measc Distillery, Tourmakeady, County Mayo

WEBSITE: loughmaskdistillery.com

DESCRIPTION: Working distillery

Distiller Eoin Holmes is gathering elderflower in the hills around Lough Measc in the wilds of Mayo. It's just one of the botanicals he and his family gather by hand to enrich the popular gin and vodka that fuel his business as he waits for his whiskey to mature. Honeysuckle and fuchsia are also stockpiled at the distillery near the lake, where his boat sits patiently, waiting for him to find time to return to fish for brown trout.

It's only ten months since he started distilling in the abandoned factory that has become the Lough Measc Distillery and it hasn't left much time for taking to the water since. His two alembic stills bring a striking beauty to the concrete walls of the building that rises up here in what he describes as one of the most beautiful places in the world. Lakes and mountains define this place and, not surprisingly, the water in his spirit is pulled straight from Lough Measc itself.

There are a few years to go before this tiny distillery reveals the double-distilled single malt that it is creating, but visitors won't be disappointed while they wait. As they pull in off the Wild Atlantic Way, they will discover a truly romantic tale of a small craft business fighting to succeed on the side of a mountain. Holmes has built a smokery behind the distillery, where he plans to smoke barley to add that rare ingredient in Irish whiskey – peat.

Lough Measc is a hand-made, traditional place, stuffed with life and big personality, with much to teach us about the value of small things.

Pearse Lyons Distillery

CONTACT: Pearse Lyons Distillery,
121–122 James Street, Dublin 8, DO8 ET27

WEBSITE: pearselyonsdistillery.com

DESCRIPTION: Boutique distillery and visitor centre.
Tours run on the hour 10am–5pm.

Locals will tell you just how incredible it is to see Pearse Lyons Distillery bring life back to St James Church in the Liberties. Left barricaded and derelict, its grounds overgrown and forgotten for decades, the grounds of this historic Dublin church contain the remains of over 100,000 people, including, reportedly, that of James Power, the founder of Powers whiskey.

When Pearse Lyons and his wife, Deirdre, chose the site, they took on board a project that most businesspeople would have run from. As it was a listed building, the restoration was so carefully completed that it included re-opening a slate mine in Wales to source material that matched the original roof tiles. Nothing was spared in its reconstruction and its beautiful re-invented glass spire now stands as a beacon of regeneration in the city.

Pearse Lyons found his success in the US with his company Alltech and said what he wanted for Dublin was to create a "new Irish whiskey with a Kentucky flair". That whiskey is double-distilled and aged in bourbon casks that come from their sister site in Lexington, Kentucky. It's a wonderful marriage of Irish emigration and return, explains master distiller Gearoid Cahill, who beams with pride as he unlocks the many stories that surround him inside the building. A boutique craft venture, its two copper stills create an amazing profile in the former altar area of the deconsecrated church.

The art of whiskey blending matters here too, Cahill explains, with the distillery using their own produced spirit, spirit from their previous distillery in Carlow, and sourced spirit from other distilleries, to create a range of whiskeys that speak to the story of this once forgotten historic landmark.

Pearse Lyons – The Original

This five-year-old blend is a smooth, easy-drinking introduction to the Pearse Lyons range. Using some of their own stock whiskey, they have blended grain and malt to create the kind of whiskey they say the people working in distilling in its historic heyday would have enjoyed. Matured in ex-bourbon barrels. Expect a light, smooth flavour, with creamy vanilla, caramel, and oak. Bottled at 42 per cent.

Pearse Lyons – Distiller's Choice

This seven-year-old is the next step along the Pearse Lyons journey. Using some of their own whiskey distilled on the stills now in Pearse Lyons, it's a blend of malt and grain whiskey. It's matured mostly in bourbon, but the master distiller has also included a smaller amount of whiskey finished in oloroso sherry casks, adding a layer of richness that sets it apart. It pairs beautifully with chocolate. Bottled at 42 per cent.

Pearse Lyons – Cooper's Select

You'll be wrapped in stories at the Pearse Lyons, none less memorable than those of the coopers in the Lyons family. Pearse's mother is said to have come from a line of coopers and it is to this profession that he gave a nod of appreciation when creating this malt and grain blended whiskey. Expect fruit to dominate, with layers of caramel and malt, while the finish is long, with dark fruits and tropical flavours mingling with oaky spice. Bottled at 42 per cent.

Pearse Lyons – Founder's Choice

With twelve years under oak, Founder's Choice is the premium end of the Pearse Lyons range. Selected by the founder himself, it's a beautifully rich single malt that comes packed with honey and summer fruits, with a warm, satisfying finish. The bar beneath the altar of the distillery is a wonderful place to try this whiskey for the first time, letting the Founder's Choice match the founder's vision around you. Bottled at 42 per cent.

Powerscourt Distillery

CONTACT: Powerscourt Distillery, Powerscourt
Estate, Enniskerry, County Wicklow,
A98 A9T7

WEBSITE: powerscourtdistillery.com

DESCRIPTION: Working distillery, visitor centre,
café/bar, and shop.
Open daily 10am–5:30pm.

The personality of the Powerscourt Distillery falls
elegantly between the wild rolling hills of Wicklow and
the famously planned gardens of the estate. A visit to
this twenty-first-century distillery, housed in an
eighteenth-century mill house, is a beautiful
experience. Exposed stone, glass, and dark wood
wrap the entrance foyer and immediately signal the
creation of a great new chapter in the Powerscourt
story. Initially conceived and developed by local
entrepreneurs Gerry Ginty and Ashley Gardiner, then
brought to life through the combined investment of
the Slazenger, Pierce, Ginty, and Gardiner families,
this young distillery has already dug deep roots into
the Irish whiskey landscape.

Not least of these is the addition of their master distiller.
Noel Sweeney spent thirty years honing his craft at

Cooley before joining Powerscourt to put his globally-recognized stamp of authority on the brand. His ambition for what they are creating here in Wicklow is infectious, and he talks with enthusiasm about the operation of the Forsyth stills, the environmental design of the distillery, the beauty of the warehousing, and, of course, the spirit they're producing.

While they wait for that very special spirit to mature, they have released the Fercullen range – a family of three whiskeys that take their cue from the Irish-language name for the landscape around them. Using Cooley stock that Sweeney helped create, he has matured and blended a trio of single grain, single malt, and a premium blend, which conjure a wonderful roadmap for the direction Powerscourt is headed and where it aims to take the Irish whiskey story next.

Fercullen Premium Blend

Malt and grain combine to create the first in the Fercullen range, a premium blend. Aged in seasoned oak, this expression of Fercullen is characterized by its vanilla and citrus notes and is a great introduction to Powerscourt. On the nose it has hints of almond and orange peel, while flavours of malt, caramel, and sweet fruit dominate the taste. It has a great vanilla and oak finish. Bottled at 40 per cent.

Fercullen 10-year-old Single Grain

After a decade spent maturing in white oak, this rare stock whiskey was recasked in fresh bourbon casks, giving it a distinctively smooth identity. There's a spice to its finish that sits easily with the vanilla, while the almond has a much richer, buttery feel. Citrus and honey dominate the nose, while layers of spicy rocket, fruit, and sweetness underpin the smooth, crisp grain flavour. It has a silky finish that's long-lasting and warm. Bottled at 40 per cent.

Fercullen 14-year-old Single Malt

There's something very rich about this fourteen-year-old single malt that sets it properly apart. Matured in bourbon barrels, it has absorbed a complex range of flavours and aromas that make it really enjoyable to drink. The honey and vanilla of the rest of the Fercullen range combine with dark fruits and cinnamon to reveal a very smooth and layered sweet malt. It's genuinely impressive and the peppered spice at its heart gives a long, lingering finish that master distiller Noel Sweeney suggests benefits from just a drop of water. Bottled at 46 per cent.

Rademon Distillery

CONTACT: Rademon Estate Distillery, Crossgar, County Down

WEBSITE: rademondistillery.com

DESCRIPTION: Working distillery and visitor centre

Just forty minutes' drive from Belfast, this craft distillery sits in a five-hundred-acre estate that has become synonymous with the idea of flavour. Its gin product, Shortcross Gin, has been a huge success, and the couple behind the venture, husband and wife David and Fiona Boyd-Armstrong, recently launched their first whiskey, which officially came of age in 2018. A single malt, it was double-distilled in 2015 and has been maturing on site, where it was bottled and labelled by hand.

Fiona Boyd-Armstrong is, at the time of writing, the only female owner and managing director of a whiskey distillery in Ireland. David Boyd-Armstrong is also the head distiller and he aims to produce a single pot still in addition to their single malt.

Rademon is one of Ireland's oldest estates, with the main house having been originally built in 1604. It is the Boyd-Armstrongs' family estate. A £2.5 million investment programme, begun in 2018, allowed the distillery to treble production overall and install a new 1,750-litre copper still, which will be dedicated to their whiskey production, while additional fermentation facilities have been added to the still house. The estate well is the source of water. A new visitor experience has been created, incorporating a bar and events space, with views across the estate.

Roe & Co Distillery

CONTACT: Roe & Co Distillery, Thomas Street, Dublin

WEBSITE: roeandcowhiskey.com

DESCRIPTION: Working distillery and visitor centre

Given how prominent it is on the Dublin skyline, it's remarkable how little is known about the green copper-domed tower neighbouring the Guinness site on Dublin's Thomas Street. This is St Patrick's Tower, the only remaining visible evidence of what was reputedly once the largest whiskey distillery in Europe. George Roe started his distilling business, George Roe & Co, here in the 1750s and St Patrick's Tower was the engine that drove it all. Now, centuries later, Diageo is bringing the Roe & Co brand back to life just up the street from the tower, in what was formerly the Guinness Power House. This striking redbrick building from the 1940s has been completely remodelled into a state-of-the-art whiskey distillery and visitor centre.

On a sneak-peek visit on the historic first day of distillation in 2019, head distiller Lora Hemy and the rest of the team are buzzing with nervous excitement. The stills are hard at work but there's plastic wrapping on the furniture and workers are putting the finishing touches to floors, walls, and ceilings of the visitor spaces in this incredibly attractive distillery.

Hemy is a young Scottish woman, bursting with creativity. She arrived in Dublin via a career that started with art college, before diverting through distilleries in Scotland, England, and Wales. She appears completely aware of the responsibility of taking on a project with so much meaning, and her creative mind is bringing the listener to a myriad of places as she talks about all the possibilities that lie ahead. It will be at least three years before she gets her hands on Roe & Co's own spirit, so for now they will use sourced whiskey to gently breathe life back into this historic brand.

Roe & Co Blended Whiskey

The first of the new premium whiskeys to emerge from Roe & Co is this blend of rich malt and smooth grain whiskey. Entirely aged in bourbon casks, it's bottled at 45 per cent. In a nod to a pear tree which is said to still grow on the original site of Roe & Co, there is a gentle fruit and spice in the finish, with creamy vanilla notes in the flavour. While it makes a great sipping whiskey on its own, Roe & Co also recommend it as a terrific cocktail base.

Royal Oak Distillery

CONTACT: Royal Oak Distillery, Carlow,
                County Carlow

WEBSITE: royaloakdistillery.com

DESCRIPTION: Working distillery

The eighteenth-century estate that is home to the Royal Oak Distillery in Carlow is an impressive place. Acres of parkland surround this modern state-of-the-art distillery, which started producing its own spirit in 2016. Owned by Italian drinks company Illva Saronno, which also owns brands like Tia Maria and Disaronno, it was originally set up in partnership with Walsh Whiskey, the maker of the award-winning and hugely popular Irishman and Writers' Tears whiskey. The two companies parted ways in 2019.

At the time of writing, visitors to the distillery could still taste and purchase the popular Walsh Whiskey products but plans are under way to bottle and brand their own as yet unnamed Royal Oak-distilled whiskey.

The distillery has become an important part of the tourism landscape along what is branded Ireland's Ancient East, a branding initiative for this part of the country to compete with the Wild Atlantic Way on the west coast. They run tours daily, which they describe as multisensory, and offer a variety of packages that take you through their triple-distilled production of pot still, malt, and grain whiskey. They distil all three types of whiskey in the one distillery building.

Slane Distillery

CONTACT: Slane Distillery, Slane, County Meath

WEBSITE: slaneirishwhiskey.com

DESCRIPTION: Working distillery and visitor centre. Tours seven days a week.

Of all the castles in Ireland, Slane probably captures the imagination most. Its history, architecture, and position at the heart of the Boyne Valley is central but, for many, it was the hosting of major international rock concerts that put the castle estate firmly in the mind's eye. Now they have opened a distillery in the grounds of the castle, giving visitors and whiskey fans a new reason to visit.

It's a great location in this historic part of Ireland's Ancient East, the lesser-known sibling to the Wild Atlantic Way, with tourism a natural part of the landscape. The Boyne Valley is rich with ancient monuments and artefacts like the megalithic tomb of Newgrange and the Hill of Tara, possibly Ireland's most important ancient site, but it's the river that cuts through it all that makes Slane so attractive.

Brown-Forman, the major US drinks corporation that also owns Jack Daniels, bought Slane Whiskey in 2015, and the Conyngham family, who first established the brand on their castle grounds, remain central. The Georgian stables have been converted to house the distillery and, along with some discreet new build, they have also opened a visitor centre. They aim for sustainability, using barley grown on the estate farm and water from the Boyne.

They have installed three pot stills and a number of column stills and are currently maturing their own spirit on site. Meanwhile, they sourced whiskey elsewhere to produce a triple-cask blend under the Slane Whiskey brand name, which has been very popular with consumers.

Slane Irish Whiskey

Three cask types are used in the blending of Slane Irish Whiskey, the flagship brand from this young distillery – virgin American oak, ex-bourbon, and ex-oloroso sherry casks. A marriage of grain and malt whiskey, it has a rich, deep flavour, derived in particular from the sherry cask that gives it an elegant feel. Expect dark fruits, spices, and caramel in the flavour, with a medium finish, which is sweet and rich. Bottled at 40 per cent.

Teeling Distillery

CONTACT: Teeling Whiskey Distillery,
13–17 Newmarket, Dublin 8

WEBSITE: teelingdistillery.com
EMAIL: reservations@teelingwhiskey.com

DESCRIPTION: Working distillery, visitor centre,
café/bar, and shop

When brothers Jack and Stephen Teeling opened the
doors to their new Dublin distillery in 2015, it was the
first new whiskey distillery in the capital in 125 years.
They chose a symbol of a phoenix as their logo,
heralding the resurgence of Dublin whiskey and also
of their family's place within the Irish whiskey story.
Their father, John Teeling, founded the Cooley
Distillery in 1987 (now owned by Beam Suntory) and
he now runs the Great Northern Distillery, supplying
sourced spirit to distilleries all over Ireland.

The phoenix logo takes pride of place on all the Teeling
products but also on the roof of the inner city distillery
they created. It's a beautiful building, inside and out,
and designed to be as effective in delivering a quality
tourist experience as it is in whiskey distillation.

Teeling's signature identity is created around innovative cask-finished blends, as well as single malt, single grain, and single pot still whiskey. Driven by US-born master distiller Alex Chasko, they have won many awards, the most notable being the title of World's Best Single Malt, awarded at the 2019 World Whiskies Awards for the Teeling 24-year-old Single Malt. This is a great achievement for such a young distillery, and a sure indicator of the direction Irish whiskey is taking on the global stage.

Teeling Distillery has proved to be an incredible engine for change, not just in the Irish whiskey industry, but also to the Liberties itself, exhibiting a confidence and pride in this inner-city quarter that it rightly deserves.

Teeling Small Batch

Teeling Small Batch is the distillery's biggest-selling bottling and was their first release under the new family brand back in February 2013. It's been an excellent champion for the company since, winning awards at home and abroad for its smooth woody undertones and great rum finish. It's a fine blend of matured grain and malt whiskey that's finished in an ex-rum cask for a further twelve months, giving it a layer of flavour that lets it stand out from the crowd. A light gold in colour, it's bottled in small batches at 46 per cent and is non-chill filtered. It's a great starting point to explore the Teeling family. Bottled at 46 per cent.

Teeling Single Grain

Single grain is a relatively new category in Irish whiskey, and one which Teeling has come to dominate, winning a number of awards since Teeling Single Grain was introduced. It finds its niche through fully maturing in ex-Californian red wine barrels, giving it a fruity, smooth flavour. Indeed, fruit has become so much a part of the description of this pale amber liquid that you'll see everything from bananas to apples to lush red berries referenced in its flavour descriptions. But there's spiciness embedded in its profile too, which makes the single grain a popular alternative to its richer single malt cousins. Bottled at 46 per cent.

Teeling Single Malt

The launch of Teeling's first single malt came with high expectations. Existing fans knew this was an opportunity for superior alchemy and budding new recruits were hoping for a single malt entry point they were familiar with. It didn't disappoint either camp. With 100 per cent malted barley from different age ranges, matured in five different wine casks (sherry, port, Madeira, white burgundy, and Cabernet Sauvignon), Teeling Single Malt created an immediately attractive flavour profile. Stuffed with personality, this non-age statement whiskey is rightly celebrated for its rich fruit flavours and layers of smooth chocolate and spice. Bottled at 46 per cent.

Teeling Single Pot Still

When Teeling Single Pot Still launched in 2018, whiskey sellers felt compelled to restrict purchases to two per customer. It was the first whiskey produced using Teeling's Dublin-produced spirit, but it had also been so long since a new single pot still had emerged in Ireland (the country that claims the category as its own) that there were fears this collector's item would be snapped up in bulk purchases. Teeling released three batches of the pot still since that launch, before settling on the final non-batched version on the shelves today. Each version has taken Teeling another step along a journey of discovering their own pot still identity. Bottled at 46 per cent.

Teeling Revival To Renaissance

The Revival, launched in the early days of the Teeling journey, was an incredibly successful series. A single malt, matured in bourbon and then finished in ex-brandy and cognac casks, it was designed to represent the return of whiskey distilling to Dublin. Now, as the distillery approaches its fifth birthday, the Revival series, having gone through five volumes, has evolved into the Renaissance, a similarly-aged Single Malt in the same characteristic bottle but with finishes that represent the future of the brand. Bottled at 46 per cent.

The Echlinville Distillery

CONTACT: The Echlinville Distillery,
62 Gransha Road, Kircubbin,
Newtownards, County Down,
Northern Ireland, BT22 1AJ

WEBSITE: echlinville.com

DESCRIPTION: Working distillery, visitor centre,
and farm

The power of the sea carved the Ards Peninsula,
creating a long finger of rich fertile land that lies
between the Irish Sea and Strangford Lough on
Northern Ireland's County Down coast. Nature
created this place apart, and the people who worked it
created a close-knit, industrious community. You'll
find The Echlinville Distillery right at its heart. As you
approach this impressive family-run farm distillery,
you'll pass among the fields that grow its barley and
see the manor house that established the Echlinville
estate in 1730. This is a true field-to-glass operation,
putting huge emphasis on having a closed-loop
production cycle that grows, malts, distils, matures,
and bottles, all on site. In fact, it is one of the only
distilleries in Ireland that floor malt their own barley.

Echlinville started distilling in 2013, laying down single malt and single pot still spirit to mature. In the years since then, and as their own spirit matures, they have used sourced whiskey to revive the Dunville Irish whiskey brand. Bringing this historic brand from a long-silent Belfast still back to life has been a tremendous success, putting the so-called Spirit of Belfast back on the world stage. They have won many international awards for their efforts and built a great foundation for the Echlinville brand itself.

Located one hour's drive from Belfast and 2.5 hours from Dublin, Echlinville are continually extending their tour experience, including converting their seventeenth-century courtyard buildings into a state-of-the-art visitor centre with tourist accommodation, a restaurant, and a museum. Existing tours include the manor house, the stillroom, the maturation warehouses, and a drink at their bar. The Echlinville is a modern, solutions-driven distillery with great personality.

Dunville's Three Crowns

The number three means everything to this vintage-inspired blend from The Echlinville. They combined three whiskeys from three different casks to create the first of the Three Crowns series: a four-year-old single grain, a ten-year-old single malt and a fifteen-year-old oloroso sherry-finished single malt. It's a sweet, smooth whiskey that strikes a careful balance between the grain and malt. Expect vanilla, caramel, and dark fruits to dominate. Bottled at 43.5 per cent.

Dunville's Three Crowns Peated

This peat-cask finished variant of Three Crowns has been lauded wherever it has been poured. Peat is a rare flavour entry on the Irish whiskey scene and, although this is quite mild in comparison to peated whiskeys elsewhere, the peat flavour is significant. With multiple awards already under its belt, it is a three-part blend of grain, single malt, and sherry-finished single malt, finished in a peated cask, which transfers the delicate peat flavour to the whiskey. Bottled at 43.5 per cent.

Dunville's PX ten-/twelve-year-old Single Malt Irish Whiskey

A multiple award winner, Dunville's Single Malt comes in two variants: a ten-year-old and a twelve-year-old. Both finished in Pedro Ximenez sherry casks, they are rich, smooth single malts. The extra time in cask for the 12-year-old allows it to develop the deep oak aroma and spicy, creamy finish even further. Full of flavour, it has a strong woody finish with citrus and orange peel layers. A drop of water opens it beautifully. Bottled at 46 per cent.

Dunville's VR PM eighteen-year-old Rum Finish Irish Whiskey

This limited-edition rum-finish eighteen-year-old is a wonderful experience. Matured in a Port Mourant Estate vintage rum cask from Guyana, it is packed with flavour. It's spicy, rich, and loaded with dark fruits and sweet rum and raisin. Look for flavours like caramel, demerara sugar, and molasses, and expect a decadent oily liquid with a quite dry finish on the palate. Bottled at cask strength, it benefits from a drop of water to release more of the vanilla and balance the black pepper. Bottled at 57.1 per cent.

The Shed Distillery

CONTACT: The Shed Distillery, Drumshanbo, County Leitrim

WEBSITE: thesheddistillery.com

DESCRIPTION: Working distillery and visitor centre

The Shed Distillery is owned by Pat J Rigney, affectionately nicknamed the Curious Mind, an entrepreneur with decades of success in the drinks industry. Following the global success of Drumshanbo Gunpowder Irish Gin, the distillery is preparing to launch its first single pot still whiskey. The Shed's pedigree in distillation has created a great launch pad for this new brand, which should be on the shelves in early 2020. With ambitions to create what Rigney calls a "premier grand cru" in the whiskey category, he says that, in addition to their triple-distilled launch version, matured in bourbon and finished in oloroso, we can expect future finishes to include Pinot Noir, Marsala, and Madeira casks.

The Shed Distillery has brought a welcome boost to this small midlands town, not just in jobs created but in a layer of prestige through its success that shines a spotlight on the region that the town deserves, he suggests. Rigney's parents met while working nearby, but he credits the local community for inspiring his loyalty in investing here. Many of the thirty staff were previously long-term unemployed with backgrounds in lots of areas, but not whiskey, he says. Rigney describes a great journey in training them in the art of distillation over the past few years, led by his head distiller, US-born Brian Taft.

The Shed will open a new visitor centre in early 2020. It will be designed around a glasshouse that celebrates the botanicals in their gin and their five copper pot stills, as well as the "hand-made" approach they take to their distillation and production. Rigney is confident it will attract tourists in search of points of difference in the whiskey category to this lesser-known part of the country, marketed as being in the Hidden Heartlands of Ireland.

Tullamore Distillery

CONTACT: Tullamore D.E.W. Visitor Centre,
Bury Quay, Tullamore, County Offaly

WEBSITE: tullamoredew.com

DESCRIPTION: Working distillery, visitor centre,
and restaurant

There are lots of trebles in the Irish whiskey story but
none more so than at Tullamore Distillery, which
produces Tullamore D.E.W., the only triple-distilled
and triple-blended Irish whiskey in Ireland. Triple-
distilled is common enough but it's the three-part
marriage of single grain, single malt, and single pot
still whiskey that gives it its edge.

Tullamore D.E.W. has a fantastic international reputation
and is the second-biggest Irish whiskey brand globally,
after Jameson. Owned by William Grant, the Scottish
drinks family invested €35 million to bring the brand
home to its own distillery in this midlands town at the
heart of Ireland. They pump their water directly from the
Slieve Bloom Mountains and distil and mature everything
on site. They've planted oak trees around the site to mark
the passage of time and, if you let them, they'll direct you
to the 400-year-old oak tree known as King Oak in the
grounds of Tullamore's Charleville Estate, for inspiration.

There's a real sense of confidence in the people you'll meet at Tullamore. They know the difference the distillery makes to the town and genuinely enjoy its success. This is not a place for heavy formality: it's a distillery stuffed with personality and revels in championing the brand's leading role in the Irish whiskey story.

Tullamore is a ninety-minute drive from Galway and Dublin, and visitors can experience either of two locations. The main visitor centre is housed in one of the original bonded warehouses along the canal in the town centre. This caters for the majority of visitors but, for the real whiskey fanatic, a backstage pass to the full working distillery just outside the town is the ultimate destination.

Tullamore D.E.W. Original

Naturally, Tullamore don't reveal the quantities of the
trio of grain, single malt, and single
pot still whiskey they use in their
recipe, but the combination makes
this entry point to their range an
incredibly smooth and easy drinking
affair. Triple-distilled and matured
in ex-bourbon and sherry casks,
Tullamore D.E.W. Original
offers lots of fresh fruit
flavours, and on the nose,
with vanilla and wood
underneath. Bottled at
40 per cent.

Tullamore D.E.W. 12-year-old Special Reserve

This complex and flavourful whiskey took double gold at the 2018 San Francisco World Spirits competition for its "deep spice flavour and robust creamy body cloaked in a definite chocolatey note". It's a wonderful whiskey that is pot still dominant while also incorporating lots of single malt and grain whiskey in the classic Tullamore trio. Matured for twelve to seventeen years in bourbon and oloroso casks, the extra share of pot still brings lots of oils, fullness, and spice. Bottled at 40 per cent.

Tullamore D.E.W. 18-year-old Single Malt

This great single malt brought home the Worldwide Whiskey Trophy – Gold Outstanding at the 2018 International Wine and Spirits Competition. A deserved winner, this is a very limited-edition whiskey matured in four casks: bourbon, sherry, port, and Madeira. Rich, warm fruit flavours combine with spice and wood to create a lingering malt sweetness. If you can't find this, then the fourteen-year-old is another great single malt in this range. Bottled at 41.3 per cent.

Tullamore D.E.W. XO Rum Cask Finish

The demerara rum cask finish is one of the most popular of Tullamore D.E.W.'s cask series, which also includes a cider cask variant. The rum cask is Caribbean, having previously matured demerara rum, and it delivers sweet tropical flavours that blend beautifully with the vanilla, wood, and fruit of the grain, single malt, and single pot still in this classic Tullamore blend. Warm spices in the finish create a lovely counterpoint to all the fruit. Bottled at 43 per cent.

Waterford Distillery

CONTACT: Waterford Distillery, Grattan Quay, Waterford

WEBSITE: waterforddistillery.ie

DESCRIPTION: Working distillery. Currently there are no formal tours but they may be available on request.

People love to talk revolution but they aren't always as eager to take action. One of a small number attempting to take a radically different approach in the Irish whiskey arena is Mark Reynier of Waterford Distillery, and his ideas are taking a firm hold here. The man behind Islay's Bruichladdich Distillery in Scotland has brought his vision of terroir and his dream of creating the "world's most profound single malt" to Waterford on Ireland's east coast.

It's a simple enough premise: instead of putting all your store in the maturation process and wood, take a fresh look at your source ingredients – the barley and grains – and where they come from. Reynier is working with multiple Irish farmers, across many different soil types, to grow and harvest barley, organic and biodynamically run, in a carefully drawn attempt to map flavour to the land it comes from. He will create so-called single-farm whiskeys, and, even though they use the same type of barley, the same wood for maturation will conjure different flavours based on the soil they've grown in. It's a radically different approach to thinking about what creates flavour.

Their first spirit was distilled in 2016 and has been maturing in French and American casks since. With the first releases due in mid 2020, the outcome of this grand experiment will be one of the most exciting unveilings of the year. If his vision is proved correct, and all indications so far would suggest they will be, the concept of terroir will become a very popular one in Irish whiskey.

West Cork Distillers

CONTACT: West Cork Distillers, Marsh Road, Skibbereen, County Cork

WEBSITE: westcorkdistillers.com

DESCRIPTION: Working distillery, tours on request

If any county in Ireland covets a sense of independence, it's Cork, and west Cork in particular. That doesn't always sit well with Dubliners but, since I'm from neither county, I've always enjoyed the competitive relationship people from these two very different places enjoy. A few short years ago, the whiskey fans of Dublin were a little suspicious of this young upstart from the southeast. Now, as West Cork Distillers enters expansion mode, they have won over their critics, with stories of their success being the main source of comment in the capital.

Founded as a microdistillery by three friends in a small fishing village in 2003, West Cork Distillers now have over seventy people employed in their new Skibbereen distillery, an established range of their own whiskey brands, and contracts with some of the biggest retailers in the country. As they forge new plans for a visitor centre, the "can-do" attitude they herald appears to have won out.

They started distilling their own spirit in 2008 and use a combination of sourced whiskey for their older product range and their own spirit for the non-age statement brands. They also produce a popular range of gin, vodka, and poitín. They take pride in the fact that much of the mashing, fermentation, and distilling equipment they use was hand-crafted on site, giving the staff a deep understanding of the technology that drives their brands. They don't run tours yet but, in keeping with their hands-on approach, they never turn anyone away, they say, so make sure to call in advance if you plan to visit.

West Cork Irish Whiskey – Bourbon cask

This is the entry-level whiskey in the West Cork Distillers' range. It's marketed as an easy-drinking blend of 75 per cent grain and 25 per cent malt. Matured in ex-bourbon barrels. Expect light vanilla, fruit, and sweetness, with a short finish. Bottled at 40 per cent.

West Cork Irish Whiskey – Cask Strength

This cask-strength whiskey started as a limited edition but quickly became part of the core range at West Cork Distillers. It's bottled at 62 per cent and the alcohol level makes an immediate claim on its personality, but fans say it's also full of flavour. A blend of 66 per cent grain and 33 per cent malt, it's matured in first-fill bourbon and then finished in exhausted whiskey casks, which the makers say allows the malt and grain to further mature and interact. Expect a smooth, spicy flavour with some floral notes.

West Cork Irish Whiskey – Black Cask

Black cask is another blended whiskey from WCD. This time they have combined 33 per cent malt and 66 per cent grain. Matured in bourbon and then finished in a double-charred cask, hence the Black Cask name, to create what they describe as an "enhanced smoothness, vanilla and a lingering sweetness". Bottled at 40 per cent.

West Cork Irish Whiskey – IPA and Stout finish

Two recent arrivals in West Cork are these beer-finished blends, both 75 per cent grain whiskey and 25 per cent malt whiskey. Each of the whiskey types was aged in bourbon casks and then after blending, finished in either a Kinsale Stout cask or a Kinsale IPA lager cask. The makers say the stout finish creates all the dark chocolate and coffee flavours you would expect from this famously dark beer, while the IPA is lighter, driving hops, roast nuts, and sweet spices in the finish. Both bottled at 40 per cent.

West Cork Irish Whiskey – Glengarriff series

The Glengarriff series focuses on single malt whiskey matured in sherry casks and then finished in one of two charred casks, using fuel from the Glengarriff forest in Cork. Furthering WCD's interest in hand-crafting tools, they worked with a local blacksmith to build a bespoke tool to help them char their casks. For the first bottling they used peat to char the casks, and for the second they used bog oak. Both of these are said to bring a layer of smokiness to the malt that is unusual for Irish whiskey. Bottled at 43 per cent.

Independent brands

Not everyone can own a whiskey distillery. Indeed, not everyone wants to. Owning a distillery must be an incredible experience – and terrifying at every turn, as you fight to keep your stills, brands, and production on track. But there is an alternative industry, and many of the bottles you'll face on Irish whiskey shelves today represent this – independent brands or whiskey bonders, who source spirit from distilleries and create their own brands.

It's nothing new – whiskey bonding and independent bottling have always been part of the Irish whiskey landscape. Pubs and grocers in every part of Ireland once had casks of whiskey delivered to their door which they then recasked, matured, blended, and bottled themselves, creating a regional variation in whiskey that was sorely lost when distilleries started to close and production and branding came under the few remaining major distillers.

Look at shop fronts on bars around Ireland today and you'll see they still proudly proclaim their whiskey bonding heritage, even though many decades may have passed since casks were rolled across their floors. Outside the bonding and bar business, working directly with a distillery to create a brand is also a growing and profitable business. Here, we take a snapshot of some bonders and bottlers, brand makers, and business people playing their own part in re-inventing the Irish whiskey landscape.

Celtic Cask Series

ASSOCIATED WITH: The Celtic Whiskey Shop

WEBSITE: celticwhiskeyshop.com

The Celtic Cask series is on one of the most exciting whiskey journeys in Ireland, led by people who really love this complicated spirit for all the right reasons. Established by Scotsman Ally Alpine and his team at the Celtic Whiskey Shop, the Cask Series manages to wrestle into each single cask that most valuable of all the ingredients in the whiskey trade – good relations. The barrels they use, the whiskey they source, the places they select for maturation – each are borne of intricate, honest, and long-standing friendships, and the forging of new ones.

Each cask in the series is named by its number in Gaelic: Celtic Cask a Haon, a Do, a Tri simply translates as Celtic Cask number one, two, and three. What's inside depends on where the whiskey was sourced, the wood that was used to mature and finish it, and how that maturation turned out. At time of writing, number 28 in the Celtic Cask series (Celtic Cask Fiche a Hocht) is on the shelves. It's a double-distilled single malt from Cooley, matured in bourbon for fourteen years and then recasked in a red burgundy cask from

Domaine Mongeard-Mugneret for over three years. Bottled at 45 per cent, it's limited to 333 bottles.

The whiskey in each individual cask could be from any of the major distilleries around the country, each bringing its own identity to the series, and the Celtic Whiskey Shop hopes to work with all the new distilleries as they emerge. Bottles in the series range from around €120 to €750, depending on age, quantity bottled, barrel type, and a particular bottle's place in the series. You could spend €12,000 buying up the entire collection, they suggest, if you could find them all. There are very few full sets of Celtic Cask around. It's thought that there might be four full sets in Ireland, not counting the collection at their sister store, the Celtic Whiskey Bar and Larder in Killarney, which has reputedly the largest private whiskey collection in Ireland. A percentage of every bottle sold is donated to charity.

Blending and bottling is a slow, expensive business that begs the question Why do they bother? Their stores already have shelves groaning with the weight of the best whiskey in the world.

They do it because it's traditional, they say, because they want to have something really special to shout about, and also because there are questions about Irish whiskey that they want to help answer. For example, does terroir really exist on an island as small as ours? Can the climatic conditions in the cask they have maturing in Dingle affect the whiskey differently from how it might turn out in their warehouse in Wexford? With so many new entrants, what will the flavour of Irish whiskey become in ten or twenty years' time? The people behind Celtic Cask want to help answer these questions and, they suggest hopefully, in doing so to drive the Irish whiskey category even higher.

Dick Mack's Pub

LOCATION: Dingle, County Kerry

WEBSITE: dickmackspub.com

A family business since it opened, the famous Dick Mack's bar in Dingle in County Kerry is run by Finn MacDonnell, the grandson of Tom MacDonnell, who opened the bar in 1899. Ready to put his own stamp on this most famous of Dingle pubs, Finn worked with Peter White to create a destination bar for whiskey drinkers. It was a superb decision, which saw Dick Mack's win Whiskey Bar of the Year multiple times since, as well as capturing the imagination of whiskey fans everywhere.

The pair have now continued their adventure with a single cask series, realized through friendships forged with distilleries around Ireland. Apart from a natural relationship with their neighbour Dingle Distillery, they have single casks under way with The Echlinville, Great Northern, Royal Oak, and even Arran in Scotland. They take great pride in the influence they have been allowed to bring on their casks to ensure that the finish and maturation realized is something truly bespoke. They are also deeply involved in the bottling and labelling of this new whiskey line.

Dick Mack's set up its own brewery in recent years in the yard behind the pub. Its success has created a natural spark of new ambition: their own small whiskey distillery. It's an exciting prospect that, like everything in the world of whiskey, we'll just have to wait for.

Glendalough Distillery

LOCATION: County Wicklow

WEBSITE: glendaloughdistillery.com

Glendalough (glen of the two lakes) is a stunning location, deeply embedded in the history and culture of Ireland. The people who created the Glendalough Distillery in the hills of County Wicklow, just south of Dublin, found a natural fit in this monastic location, as they built this boutique operation into a strong Irish brand with an international outlook. They already produce a gin and a poitín, and they have recently brought life to their whiskey stills, preparing to distil their own pot still whiskey.

Until now, they have used sourced whiskey to produce a range of award-winning brands, which have captured the imagination with their range of finishes. All matured in bourbon, each of their range has been further finished in a carefully selected series of casks, such as their seven-year-old single malt with a craft porter cask finish or their limited edition thirteen-year-old single malt with a Japanese minuzara finish, a first for Irish whiskey.

Flavour and innovation matter to these whiskey champions, and their adventures in Irish oak are the strongest indicator of this. Native Irish oak is one of the rarest woods in Ireland today, and so, to work with it on whiskey casks is a special experience. Glendalough took fourteen oak trees, replacing each with seven new saplings, to produce casks with wood that originates within walking distance of the distillery. These casks were then used to finish a 25-year-old single malt. It's an ambitious and hugely attractive project, which will produce bottles numbered to the tree the cask came from, and visitors to Glendalough will, in time, be able to visit the location in which the tree grew.

Grace O'Malley Irish Whiskey

WEBSITE: graceomalleywhiskey.com

It's fascinating to watch a new brand take shape, particularly one built on a reputation as powerful as Grace O'Malley, a historic character known as the pirate queen, renowned along the western seaboard in the mid-1500s. I met the people behind this new brand in the Dingle Whiskey Bar in Dublin. We were there to taste the Captain's range, the ultra-premium slice of a three-tier whiskey collection under the Grace O'Malley name. Created by Mayo businessman Stephen Cope and two German entrepreneurs, Stefan Hansen and Hendrick Melle, another international layer was added with the introduction of French cellar master and blender, Paul Caris.

Caris is excited about what we're about to taste: Grace O'Malley 18-year-old Single Malt Amarone Cask. This eighteen-year-old double-distilled single malt is taken from Cooley stock that has been finished in Italian Amarone casks. Amarone is a rich, intense red wine produced near Verona and is one of a trio of cask finishes under the Captain's range, along with cognac and port. The Amarone finish is a wonderful experience, the Cooley whiskey making a superb base for the rich, dark fruit and spiced vanilla layers. You'll pay for it, though, and so, thankfully, the people behind Grace O'Malley have introduced two additional entry points alongside the premium Captain's range: Navigator (mid-range) and Crew (entry level).

The brand's flagship whiskey is simply Grace O'Malley Irish whiskey and that sits comfortably under the Crew title. A blend of grain and malt, it is matured in bourbon and combines multiple batches of whiskey of varying age statements from three to ten years old. The resulting blend delivers a whiskey balanced between fruitiness, age character, complexity, and smoothness. The mid-range Navigator includes the Grace O'Malley Dark Char and Rum Cask edition. This blend of grain and malt whiskey is aged in bourbon before its rum cask finish.

JJ Corry

ASSOCIATED WITH: Chapelgate Whiskey

WEBSITE: chapelgatewhiskey.com

The release of the world's first tequila- and mezcal-finished Irish whiskey is probably the best starting point to get to know the people behind the JJ Corry brand. It evokes exactly the kind of sit-up-and-take-notice effect that its creator Louise McGuane was looking for when she set her sights on bringing the art of blending back to her native County Clare. Called the Battalion, the whiskey was inspired by the San Patricios, a group of Irish soldiers who fought on the side of Mexico during the Mexican/American war of 1846–48. Batch one comprised only seven hundred bottles of this blend of nine-year-old grain and thirteen-year-old malt whiskey.

McGuane has a background in the drinks industry which has allowed her to bring an international perspective to the rural place where she grew up. Her company, Chapelgate Whiskey, with its bonded rackhouse, is across the road from where her father still grazes cattle, and near the village where the brand's namesake, JJ Corry, once blended his own whiskey.

It's a small-scale operation with big ambition. Set up in 2017, the brand is firmly in the scale-up phase, with logistics and sales teams pushing the brand across the USA, the UK, and beyond. They have two additional brands. The Gael, their first bottling, is a triple blend of twenty-six-year-old, eleven-year-old, and fifteen-year-old single malt with a seven-year-old grain. The second is the Flintlock, a sixteen-year-old single malt.

Knappogue Castle

ASSOCIATED WITH: Castle Brands

WEBSITE: knappoguewhiskey.com

Knappogue Castle is one of those Irish whiskeys that is forever tied to the USA. It emerged from the private collection of Texan businessman Mark Edwin Andrews, who, with his wife, bought and restored the fifteenth-century Knappogue Castle in County Clare in 1966. As the restoration of the tower house progressed, Andrews bought up casks of maturing whiskey for a private collection, eventually bottling it under the Knappogue Castle label.

All Knappogue Castle whiskey is sourced. They don't own their own distillery and are fiercely proud of this independent status. Their marketing of Knappogue in the USA, Ireland, and beyond has been hugely successful. Now owned by Castle Brands, a company established by the label founder's son, Mark Edwards III, it has a core range of three age-statement single malts, a cask series, and the much-lauded Knappogue 1951, a thirty-one-year-old vintage sherry-cask-aged single malt.

The three core bottles are Knappogue 12-year-old, a 14-year-old, and a 16-year-old single malt, each triple-distilled and matured in bourbon, with variations in age and wood bringing different layers of complexity to each. The fourteen-year-old, aged in both bourbon and sherry casks, won overall Irish Whiskey of the Year at the Irish Whiskey Awards in 2016, a fantastic result for an independent brand.

Watch out also for the Knappogue 21-year-old limited edition, a splendid marriage of two single malts of twenty-one and twenty-three years and their latest Cask Finish Series. This features their classic twelve-year-old single malt, finished in French oak casks from Bordeaux winery, Château Pichon Baron, and featuring burgundy, Marsala, and the incredibly complex Marchesi Di Barolo wine cask finishes.

Paddy whiskey

ASSOCIATED WITH: Sazerac

The first time I realized Paddy was a whiskey deserving of more attention was when I ended up on a workshop in Midleton Distillery with a group of French bar and restaurant owners and staff. I was surprised to hear that they had travelled to Cork to learn more about this incredibly mellow whiskey that their customers had come to love. I was fascinated to hear how well this whiskey brand had travelled and indeed to learn that it was the fourth best-selling Irish whiskey globally, with fans all over the world.

This was before US drinks giant Sazerac bought the brand from Irish Distillers (who still make Paddy in Cork on their behalf). It's a classic Irish whiskey, its name emerging from the lived experience of charismatic salesman Paddy Flaherty, and not a marketing spin, as many people imagine. Originally a seven-year-old pot still, Paddy has since evolved into a triple-distilled blend of grain, pot still, and malt whiskey, and bottled at 40 per cent.

Matured in bourbon barrels and sherry butts, Paddy has a fresh floral nose with vanilla and honey. It has a soft malt flavour, with a distinct woody character. Its finish is described as relaxed and mellow.

Silkie

ASSOCIATED WITH: Sliabh Liag Distillers,
County Donegal

WEBSITE: www.sliabhliag.com

The Sliabh Liag (Slieve League) cliffs are a wild and rugged place, the highest sea cliffs in the country. Although they are not as well known as the cliffs of Moher, their County Donegal location is one of the most dramatic in Ireland. Hidden in the hills behind them is a gin distillery that makes An Dulaman gin, a maritime-themed gin that includes five different types of seaweed, as well as other botanicals. They also produce a whiskey called Silkie that uses sourced whiskey, as they wait to open their own whiskey distillery on a site in nearby Adara. A Donegal whiskey distillery will be a hugely welcome addition to the Irish whiskey scene when it does open, as the county has a long and rich connection with whiskey and poitín making.

Naturally, in the absence of a whiskey distillery, Silkie is sourced from outside Donegal, but has been wrapped up in local lore that suits its re-invention. The Silkies were fabled shape-shifting creatures from the sea who on land transformed into beautiful women. The whiskey named after them is a blend of malt and grain with a signature smooth and easy-drinking appeal. It's a sweet honey-flavoured spirit with hints of malt and biscuit and an elegant smooth finish.

Sliabh Liag hope to create a series of triple-distilled single malt and pot still whiskeys when their distillery does get under way in the future, with a hoped-for smoky finish that would make perfect sense in this northern county, with its strong Scottish connections.

Sonny Molloy's

ASSOCIATED WITH: The Front Door

WEBSITE: frontdoorpub.com

A whiskey bar in Galway is hard to beat. The combination of west of Ireland hospitality, a roaring fire, and a great whiskey is a recipe that has fuelled many a night in this most social of Irish cities. Sonny Molloy's whiskey bar sits at the heart of it all on High Street. The pub has brought renewed life to the site of this former drapery shop, which was run by the popular and larger-than-life character Sonny Molloy himself. His original dark-wood shop counter takes pride of place in the pub today and functions as the bar counter.

Naturally, this whiskey bar nestled within the larger Front Door pub, has a fantastic collection of whiskey, and one of their crown jewels is the full collection of Midleton VR on display behind glass, one of the few full collections of this very special whiskey in a bar in Ireland. But fighting for a slice of the limelight since late 2018 is their own Sonny Molloy's single cask of sixteen-year-old Redbreast. Just 570 bottles of this incredibly rich and full-bodied whiskey were taken from its 500-litre Spanish oak cask, with just two hundred of these being released for general sale.

The rest will be served by the glass across Sonny's counter.

This is a wonderfully complicated and spicy whiskey, stuffed with personality. It takes all the great qualities of this most famous of single pot stills and layers dark nuts, chocolate, and pepper among its sweet and honeyed flavour. It has a deep, long finish that celebrates its sherry origins and delivers a wonderful sense of fullness.

The Friend at Hand

ASSOCIATED WITH: Whiskey Museum and Shop, Belfast

WEBSITE: dukeofyorkbelfast.com

Storytelling counts at The Friend at Hand, the whiskey museum and shop at the heart of Belfast's Titanic Quarter. And the person most likely to be regaling the crowd will be Willie Jack, the London School of Economics graduate who owns The Friend at Hand, as well as the neighbouring Duke of York, Harp Bar, and others in this thriving city district. The Duke of York, stuffed to the rafters with memorabilia itself, has been voted the best whiskey bar in Ulster numerous times.

As well as the six hundred whiskeys in The Friend at Hand, half of which will never be sold, Willie Jack has also created his own series of thirteen-year-old single malts, sourced from a Northern Irish distillery. Together they make up a (currently) nine-part gallop through Willie Jack's imagination. With titles like Pride not Prejudice, the Dark Horse, and Girona Gold & the Missing Rubies, each hand-numbered and signed bottle comes with a rollicking good story ahead of its tasting note.

The Friend at Hand has also produced three single-cask bottlings: a fourteen-year-old Powers; a twenty-five-year-old Redbreast, and a twenty-year-old Midleton.

The Friend at Hand and the rest of the businesses anchored to the flagship Duke of York bar form an incredibly attractive draw in this exciting young city. If you visit Belfast and don't get further than this lavish collection of hostelries, don't worry. Everyone will understand.

The Long Hall

ASSOCIATED WITH: Powers

CONTACT: The Long Hall, 51 South Great George's Street, Dublin 2

When The Long Hall in Dublin, one of the capital's most elegant Victorian bars, set out to mark its 250 years in business, it looked to Powers whiskey for companionship. It's no surprise: the two have spent centuries in each other's company, with the bar being just twenty-five years old when James Power founded the famous distillery nearby. To mark those first 250 years, Marcus Houlihan, who is the current custodian of this beautiful hostelry on Dublin's George's Street, launched Powers The Long Hall Single Cask Release. It bears all the hallmark spicy flavours of Powers, layered with the creamy mouth feel characteristic of Irish pot still whiskey.

It's a rich complex experience, which bears testimony to the location. The Long Hall was refurbished in 1881, and the opulent bar, layout, and gold-painted mirrors installed then remain in place today, catching the reflection of countless guests through the decades. Marcus Houlihan's parents took over as custodians of the bar in May 1972. Always looking forward, their son

Marcus became a Founding Father of the Dingle Distillery and has a single cask maturing in the wilds of Kerry that he will bottle in 2022, to mark his parents' fiftieth anniversary in the pub.

Until then, there is a limited number of bottles of the Powers single cask left and, once it reaches the fifty-bottle mark, Marcus will stop selling it by the bottle to ensure he has plenty to sell by the glass for years to come. Try a glass at the bar soon. It's a truly exclusive experience.

The Palace Bar

CONTACT: The Palace Bar, Fleet Street, Dublin 2

When the Ahern family bought the Victorian Palace Bar in Dublin from the widow Ryan in the late 1940s, the art of blending whiskey was already in full swing. Never a family to be out of step with fashion, they almost immediately started bottling their own label, laying the foundation for the bar's reputation today as a champion of Irish whiskey. Their first-floor whiskey bar, the Whiskey Palace, is a destination in itself, but it's their return to blending that confirms their place as leaders in the Dublin whiskey renaissance.

Willie Ahern, the current proprietor, started his journey back to blending by re-introducing the Palace Bar own label, a four-part family of nine-, twelve-, and fourteen-year-old single malt whiskeys embedded in the literary and journalistic history of the bar. Now they have taken that whiskey journey a step further by collaborating with individual distilleries on single-cask releases of some incredible whiskey.

Their Redbreast seventeen-year-old all-sherry single cask is a triumph. Bottled at cask strength of 57.9 per cent, it was the culmination of an arduous process of selection that yielded some 540 bottles. The complexity of this collaboration is not a surprise: Redbreast itself is a singular mark of character in Irish whiskey, and forging an alliance with the Palace Bar doubled the demand for excellence.

They also recently released a single-cask collaboration with Dingle Distillery, the first bar to release one of the Dingle Founding Father casks. Not all the bottles of this 58.6 per cent single-malt five-year-old oloroso sherry cask will sell by the bottle. A proportion are being held back for serving to customers by the glass.

Tipperary Boutique Distillery

ASSOCIATED WITH: Jennifer Nickerson, Stuart Nickerson, and Liam Aherne

WEBSITE: tipperarydistillery.ie

Jennifer Nickerson grew up around whiskey. With her family, she spent her formative years following her father Stuart as he moved around the Scottish distilleries he managed, taking in the sights, smells, and sounds of this burgeoning industry. It's a lifestyle that has stayed with her, and now, nestled among the fields and hills of rural Tipperary, she joins her father and husband at the helm of a new whiskey brand, Tipperary Whiskey Distillery.

The distillery in their name is a "project in planning" and, as they wait for their own stills to spring to life, they've launched an independent brand of whiskey using sourced whiskey from other distilleries, all under the Tipperary name.

Based on husband Liam Aherne's family farm, the whiskey company's trio of independently bottled whiskeys champion the landscape and history around them. The Rising, an eleven-year-old single malt, was launched to mark one hundred years since Ireland's

Easter Rising; the Watershed, a non-age statement single malt references the water from their farm in Ballindoney that is used to cut it to 47 per cent; the Knockmealdowns is named after the mountain range that straddles the Tipperary and Waterford border and overlooks their farm.

Walsh Whiskey

ASSOCIATED WITH: Bernard and Rosemary Walsh

WEBSITE: walshwhiskey.com

When Sweny's Pharmacy, the celebrated Dublin venue that features in James Joyce's *Ulysses*, was under threat of closure in 2019, due to massively rising rents, it was Walsh Whiskey that stepped into the breach. Walsh's entrepreneurial founders, Bernard and Rosemary Walsh, paid a significant contribution towards their rent and are helping the volunteer-run literary landmark forge a financial future. It was a kind gesture in a difficult year that saw the brand split from their business partners, the Italian drinks giant Illva Saronno, requiring them to walk away from the Royal Oak Distillery that they had built together in County Carlow but, crucially, allowing Walsh to retain its brands.

These brands are the Irishman and Writers' Tears, two whiskeys that couldn't be more perfectly named for an international market in love with all things Irish and literary. They have found legions of fans and multiple awards for their master blends of triple-distilled single-malt and pot still whiskeys. The Irishman range includes twelve-year-old, seventeen-year-old, and a Marsala cask finish single malt, while Writers' Tears

comes in six variants – Writers' Tears
Copper Pot; Double Oak, an American
and French oak double casking; an Italian
Marsala cask finish; Pot Deau XO,
a super-premium cognac finish;
Red Head, a Spanish oloroso sherry
finish; and Writers' Tears
cask strength,
bottled at
53 per cent.

Index

Picture Credits

The publishers would like to thank the following for their assistance with images:

Ballykeefe Distillery, Blackwater Distillery, Boann Distillery, Bushmills Distillery, Clonakilty Distillery, Connacht Distillery, Dingle Distillery, Dublin Liberties Distillery, Irish Distillers, Kilbeggan Distillery, Killowen Distillery, Lough Measc Distillery, Pearse Lyons Distillery, Powerscourt Distillery, Rademon Distillery, Roe & Co Distillery, Royal Oak Distillery, Slane Distillery, Teeling Distillery, The Echlinville Distillery, Tullamore Distillery, West Cork Distillery

Celtic Whiskey Shop, Dick Mack's Pub, Glendalough Distillery, Grace O'Malley Whiskey, Chapelgate Whiskey, Knappogue Whiskey, Sazerac, Sliabh Liag Distillers, Front Door Pub, The Friend at Hand, The Long Hall, The Palace Bar, Tipperary Distillery, Walsh Whiskey

Irish Whiskey Magazine

Gary Quinn